Conversing With Paradise

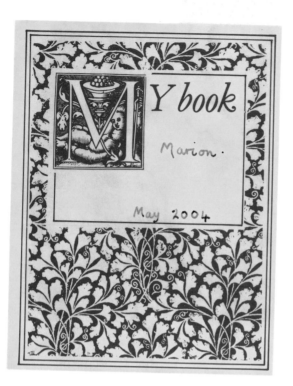

MY book

Marion.

May 2004

Conversing With Paradise

BRIAN KEEBLE

GOLGONOOZA PRESS

First published by Golgonooza Press
3 Cambridge Drive, Ipswich IP2 9EP, UK

Copyright © Brian Keeble 2003

British Library Cataloguing-in-Publication Data
A catalogue record of this book is available
from the British Library

ISBN 0 903880 77 6 *cloth*
ISBN 0 903880 78 4 *paper*

Typeset by Dave Etheridge
Printed by Smith Settle

FOR JANET
IN ETERNAL MEMORY

Contents

Preface

THIS collection of what are separate essays, but are here revised to bring them into their present alignment, might well bear the sub-title, Studies in Poetry and Traditional Wisdom. Certainly they chart unfashionable territory. At a time when poetry has little regard for anything beyond the commonplace realities of everyday perception and sentiment, these studies, in effect, propose a restoration of balance as between outer and inner worlds. For too long, in the wake of our attempt at a rational, scientific civilisation, it has been readily assumed that the centre of gravity of reality falls within the realm of the physical world. Indeed, is the operation of the laws that govern that world. But for the poets discussed in these pages the opposite is the case. For them the centre of gravity of the Real and the True decidedly falls within the spiritual world, the 'other', 'hidden' domain which has immemorially been the source of enduring values and meanings. So, in the nature of things, it must remain.

The first three essays are intended to give some cultural and imagin-ative focus to the more specific studies that follow. It is not a question of making a case for these poets as being inspired mystics or visionaries (though they are hardly without inspiration and vision). It is more a question of discerning to what extent they participate imaginatively in the realities of Spirit made comprehensible by the revealed traditions. We do not turn to poets for the formulation of doctrine and principle, but we might yet find from their work resonances of the True in the beauties of measured speech and how we are even now among inti-mations of the abiding good in the human condition. Blake wrote in his *Vision of the Last Judgment*, 'Poetry, Painting and Music, the three Powers in Man of conversing with Paradise, which the flood did not Sweep away'. What these poets have in common is that they invoke an image of man as being only fully human insofar as he can attach himself to realities which transcend the human state as such. In this sense they speak in accordance with that mode of timeless wisdom that has been called the *sophia perennis*.

It is part of the contention of these pages that, if the imaginative vision of these poets belongs to an outmoded cultural phrase, if they are perceived to be trafficking in a knowledge that has been superseded, then it follows that most of the culture of the past must now the jettisoned as one would any obsolete junk. Spiritually, the reckoning is that decisive. Now that the ruins of a failed, secular culture are everywhere evident, the imaginative vision of these poets can renew and refresh our perception of the human vocation; what we are called to be and do. In probing beneath the surface of the poetry I must hope I have not destroyed for the reader its 'artistic' value. In any case, it is integral to my viewpoint that the former does not necessarily entail the latter.

As the years of a life accumulate so the extent of one's indebtedness grows. These studies, as any I am likely to write, owe much to the work of René Guénon, A. K. Coomaraswamy and Frithjof Schuon and the group of writers associated with them. Over many years and a great many hours of conversation and reading her work, Kathleen Raine has added to my indebtedness—one I am privileged to acknowledge. I would like to thank Jenny McCosh and James Wetmore for their help in preparing a final text. I especially want to thank Wendell Berry, who read my first draft (but not its last chapter) with patience and precision and challenged me on almost every page to do better. What the text subsequently became may not entirely please him. I know it is immeasurably better for his intervention. Faults that remain are, of course, those of the author. The dedication is meant to pay tribute to one whom, I have come to see, made much of the original work possible.

I am grateful to the following journals for permission to use material that first appeared in their pages: *Agenda, Temenos, Thames Poetry, The Sewanee Review, Sophia Perennis, Studies in Comparative Religion* and *Studies in Mystical Literature.*

I

A Time of Darkness

Nothing but truth itself can be the exact measure of truth.
Nicholas of Cusa

IN RECENT CENTURIES IT HAS BEEN THE NORM FOR CRITICAL
philosophy to turn its back on the doctrines of metaphysics, assuming, quite rightly, that they have little or nothing to offer a dialectic more or less entrenched in its materialist assumptions. But in recent years it has become apparent to a generation impatient with the sterility and impotence of academic philosophy that there is much in the sacred traditions of both the West and the East that might offer a way out of the impasse that modern philosophical thought seems to have created.

The disparity between modern philosophy and the metaphysical doctrines of the sacred traditions follows on from what the Renaissance instituted, namely, a gradual isolation of knowledge from the spiritual. As a result we have what amounts to an abandonment of those criteria which safeguard against the dangers of developing human knowledge in isolation from metaphysical truth. The ontological status of knowledge has been impoverished so as to preclude, in the act of knowing, the spiritual regeneration of the knower. In this—in effect the indissoluble duality of knower and known—the problem of the ultimate nature of intellect is expressly shelved.

That philosophy in the West has considered the discourse of metaphysics as meaningless, is only the logical outcome of attempting to build a philosophy of being, not on the first principles of metaphysical certainty, but on the partiality and findings of the empirical, quantitative sciences. To this extent critical philosophy has proven itself largely unable to avoid the pitfall of all relativism—that of positing as an 'absolute' truth that nothing but the relatively true exists.

All this points to the need to reaffirm the true nature of the metaphysical since, as René Guénon has pointed out, there is nothing from which the metaphysical dimension is absent and only by recourse to its permanent principles can contingent and relative domains of thought find their orientation in relation to truth. Certainly we cannot afford to confuse metaphysics as understood by modern critical philosophy with the metaphysic that is the subject of the metaphysical traditions of the East and of the scholastic West.[1] An examination of the concept 'metaphysics' and its relation to the decline of western culture may not then be untimely.

> Metaphysic is the knowledge of the universal principles on which all things necessarily depend, directly or indirectly; in the absence of metaphysic, any other knowledge, of whatever order it may be, is literally lacking in principle, and if by that it gains a little in independence (not as a right, but as a matter of fact), it loses much more in import and depth. That is why western science is, as it were, all on the surface. While scattering its energies among countless fragments of knowledge, and losing its way among the innumerable details of fact, it learns nothing about the true nature of things, which it declares to be inaccessible in order to justify its powerlessness in this respect.[2]

Here Guénon pin-points the paradox of the materialist mentality which is largely responsible for the present character of western culture and civilisation. While by its methods it must declare truth to be unknowable, intelligence must none the less proceed on the assumption that truth is the logical and ultimate end of all its operations. In consequence, no answers are forthcoming that entirely satisfy the need for an ultimate knowledge as to the nature of the Real, of man and of human destiny. Such questions remain seemingly insoluble, or, when posed, elicit only superficial and incomplete answers in the rationalist context from which they arise. The prodigious efforts of virtuosity that comprise the intellectual history of the West during the last five centuries are surely indicative of an anguished desire for certitude on the part of man, an enquiry which is symptomatic of his dispossession as the central intelligence in the order of created beings.

If the scientist feels some justification in upbraiding the metaphysician for his lack of 'proof' he nevertheless has to admit that his own speculations are founded upon assumptions that cannot be verified absolutely. That man's intelligence is never satisfied with less than truth suggests that intelligence itself has essentially something in common with the Absolute. If there is no certainty in knowledge, why think; if there is certainty in knowledge that is proof that intelligence has something in common with Truth—the absolute identity of knowing and Being. At its ontological and intuitive roots, the function of intelligence is to distinguish between the Real and the illusory, the permanent and impermanent, and this is not possible so long as human knowledge is developed in isolation from the sapiential doctrines of a tradition. Every tradition stems from a revelation and is, as Seyyed Hossein Nasr has stated, both *the* religion and *a* religion. That is to say it possesses, inherently, the Truth and the means of attaining the Truth. This integral spirituality of a tradition will emphasise a particular perspective of Truth according to the spiritual and psychological needs of the section of humanity whose destiny it shapes. But insofar as a tradition contains the objective manifestations of the Spirit it offers the possibility of an adequate re-presentation of the Absolute, so that we are justified in considering its metaphysical principles as the ultimate referent of all spiritual and intellectual experience. The essential identity between the Absolute and intelligence provides not only the principial orientation for all modes of intellection but also the objective criteria for the contingent truths of discursive thought. For the intelligence to fully understand one thing it must needs have some grasp of the intelligible itself: that is intellectual intuition, which implies the comprehension of Being in itself as well as in connection with things.

Like a container, like content, and vice versa: in nature a container is made for a corresponding content and proves the reality of the latter, indicating that such proof, though not necessary to every understanding, has its secondary and provisional utility. A human womb proves the existence of the human seed ... similarly, human intellect proves its essential and total content, namely absolute and therefore transcendent Reality and, together therewith, the reverberations of the Absolute in the contingent.[3]

The part cannot be fully understood without the whole, for any part involves the whole. The very 'act' of intuition participates in the intelligible *form* of the totality of possibilities—the *form* of all things conformable. Truth is inconceivably yet paradoxically conceived in every conception. Intuition is not an object of knowledge open to the scrutiny of the rational mind, but is the ground upon which any necessity to give an intellectual account of things must proceed. In the unmanifest essence of intuition inheres every ultimate criteria and value of human knowledge. From this essence all modes of knowledge derive their reality.

As to the term *metaphysics* it is of the utmost importance that we do not have in mind here the metaphysics of such philosophers as Descartes, Spinoza, Kant or any modern philosophical system. For these, metaphysics constitutes an attempt at a systematic explanation of all that lies beyond facts—in other words it attempts by discursive means to encompass that which makes rational thought possible. Thus for the rationalist philosopher metaphysics, rather than being any particular field of thought, is a wisdom about thinking, 'an analysis of what it means to think, and an enquiry as to what may be the ultimate reference of thought'. Being rational in its operation, it can never transcend 'thinking' as such. Moreover, this philosophic metaphysics,

or human wisdom about things known or knowable, must be systematic, since it is required by hypothesis that its perfection will consist in an accounting for everything, in a perfect fitting together of all the parts of the puzzle to make one logical whole; and the system must be a *closed* system, one namely limited to the field of time and space, cause and effect, for it is by hypothesis about knowable and determinate things, all of which are presented to the cognitive faculty in the guise of effects, for which causes are sought.[4]

It would also be a mistake to think of metaphysics as the principle of knowledge, for it is not that all knowledge is deduced analytically from it but rather that it is the apprehension of a reality prior to thoughts or even 'thinking'. Just as the eye cannot see sight so we cannot attempt an explanation of vision by means of the objects we see. Any attempt to yoke metaphysics to philosophy in a systematic, discussive manner cannot escape the fundamental error of deducing Being from thought itself. To annex the transcendent truths of metaphysics proper to philosophical thinking is to substitute a theory of knowledge for knowledge itself.

The word itself gives the clue to its meaning, which is the knowledge of what is 'beyond' (meta) 'nature' (physis) – that is, the intuited essence of experience itself before we ascertain the nature of *what is* experienced. Being essentially constituted by that which is 'beyond physics', the metaphysical is limitless and universal, and is by that fact properly speaking incommunicable except by means of the analogical discourse of myth, symbol and ritual. Accordingly every other point of view other than the metaphysical is more or less partial and specialised and therefore subject to certain limitations. This is true of theology as well as of science and philosophy. Even during the Scholastic Middle Ages, metaphysics came to be treated as being dependent upon theology. The primary function of Scholasticism was to combat error rather than provide a means of contemplation and realisation. Although metaphysics must at all times presupposes the essential unity and oneness of Being, none the less,

pure being is neither the first nor the most universal principle, for it

17

is already a determination. It is thus necessary to go beyond being, and it is this that is of the greatest significance. That is why in all true metaphysical conceptions it is necessary to take into account the inexpressible; just as everything that can be expressed is literally nothing in comparison with that which surpasses expression, so the finite, whatever its magnitude, is nothing when faced with the Infinite. One can hint at much more than can be experienced, and this is the part played by exterior forms. All forms, whether it is a matter of words or symbols, act only as a support, a fulcrum for rising to possibilities of conception that far outstrip them.[5]

That the empirical sciences cannot provide such 'possibilities of conception' should be obvious. Whenever the modern rationalist mentality, operating more often than not on the basis of its empirical knowledge, wishes to establish first principles, it is forced to do so in terms of conceptions of reality and truth already coloured by its own mental products. This characteristic of the modern mind has dogged the West ever since Descartes envisaged Universal Being in terms of a private awareness of one's own seperate existence. Here, the appeal to 'truth' becomes, in effect, an appeal to the objectivity of the subjective experience of phenomena. This fails to see that the experience of phenomenal knowledge is a form of mentation that takes for granted its own indefinable and non-discursive essence,

> the reality of which has been consistently denied by modern philosophy, which has failed to grasp its real nature whenever it has not preferred simply to ignore it; this faculty can also be called the pure intellect, following the practice of Aristotle and his Scholastic successors, for to them the intellect was in fact that faculty which possessed a direct knowledge of principles. Aristotle expressly declares [*Posterior Analytics*, Book II] that 'the intellect is truer than science', which amounts to saying that it is more true than the reason which constructs that science; he also says that 'nothing is more true than the intellect', for it is necessarily infallible from the fact that its

operation is immediate and because, not being really distinct from its object, it is identified with the truth itself.[6]

A culture whose tacit conception of being derives from the forms and modes of reflexive knowledge and which denies the immediate and intellectual nature of the metaphysical, will in practice insists that art is the object of the secondary faculties of 'emotion' and 'feeling'. Ours is perhaps the first culture to value independently and for their own sake the incidental aesthetic, emotional qualities of the auditory, tactile and visual elements that are properly the *means* of art. In so doing, we appear to have relinquished the right to enquire of a work of art whether it is good or bad without first knowing 'about' or 'of' what it may be good or bad. In such a context, the idea that the various arts can be conceived as an analogical discourse in which Truth is embodied and reflected according to the nature of the activity of art itself must seem, to say the least, far-fetched. But only by such means can human creativity have an effective and living relationship to Truth. In any culture based upon the meaning and value of the Sacred, through a qualitative cosmology, the contingencies of human existence are at all times orientated towards assimilation of the Sacred as the ultimate reference of any human activity or aspiration. This being so, at any point in time or space an individual's existence can be symbolically related to two presiding ideas: that of its sacred *centre* and that of its spiritual *origin*.

This, the metaphysical view as one might call it, acknowledges that, as the *disposition* by which we make things by the aid of a true rule (Aristotle),[7] art in all its modes of making and doing, is the application and extension of principles which must be subject to the criteria of the intellect. This implies that, for the artist, immersion in the purely personal and individual for its own sake is meaningless when the subjective as such cannot be situated within a context relating it to the destiny of the whole man—body, soul and spirit. For the artist so situated, art is the making manifest of that which is at once 'hidden' and 'revealed' in the cosmos—it is to render the events of this human life after the 'model' of an archetypal world of the Spirit. That is, for traditional man 'neither the objects of the external world nor human acts, properly speaking, have any autonomous intrinsic value. Objects or acts acquire a value, and in so doing become real, because they participate after one fashion or another, in a reality that transcends them.[8]

The analogical cosmologies that are the qualitative discourse of the sacred traditions are the only properly comprehensive re-presentation of the Sacred since, in the integrality of the tradition in question, they are rooted in the Divine Principle itself. Functioning within the spiritual context of such a traditional cosmology intelligence participates in the essential reality of the Cosmos. In this way, what man is and does is experienced in a paradigmatic fashion that contributes to the regeneration of the primordial Unity of all things. By disregarding metaphysical intuition, modern man's thought is cut off from the modes of reality by which it could attain to an apprehension of the creation and man's place in it as the interplay of theophanic energies. That is to say, of experiencing the creation, in all its variagated wonders as the expression of a redemptive cosmic environment. It is further to say that modern man lacks any guide that would lead him to a point from which time and space can be seen to be metaphysically 'unreal' when experienced as anything other than the projection of a timeless Now without extension and duration.

Such a moment, paradoxical to common experience, can be known by means of the mediating symbol—whether in the formal symbol itself, in ritual—that is 'symbol in action'—or in the 'crystalised' archetypal experience of mythical structures. The analogical language of these symbolic perspectives prepares us for the regenerative experience of the sacred. Traditionally, man, created in the divine image, does not identify himself with his psycho-physical being. For him, as Mircea Eliade has written,

An object or an act becomes real only insofar as it imitates or repeats an archetype. Thus, reality is acquired solely through repetition or participation; everything which lacks an exemplary model is 'meaningless', i.e. it lacks reality. Men would thus have a tendency to become archetypal and paradigmatic. This tendency may well appear paradoxical, in the sense that the man of a traditional culture sees himself as real only to the extent that he ceases to be himself (for a modern observer) and is satisfied with imitating and repeating the gestures of another, In other words, he sees himself as real. i.e., as 'truly himself', only, and precisely, insofar as he ceases to be so.[9]

In contrast, modern man, inasmuch as he is the embodiment of his own theoretical construct of himself, can only postulate his 'self' by means of the interaction of his bodily experience with his psychological personality. But at any given moment his personality, as a postulation, is no more than a sequence of observed behaviours linked to form a continuum that he thinks of as 'himself'. But in such a continuum he is always becoming something else and so his identity, *who* he is, has no permanence, except in a very conditional sense. Only in the non-discursive essence of intellect can man be said to participate in what is immutably real, and therefore unconditionally true—a truth that is both metaphysically and logically the prior reality and ground of every thing that 'was' or 'is to come'. We recall Aristotle: 'Nothing is more true than the intellect'. Eternity is more true than time since time is a projection or moving image of the Eternity from which it derives its reality. Time can only proceed on the basis of a stasis that alone could give meaning to the notion of a 'beginning of Time'—a presence altogether beyond even an indefinite extension of duration. Intuition itself shares in this relationship in that, being infallibly and immediately identifiable with Truth—the eternal moment that is Now—it forms of necessity the absolute stasis on which the contingent existence of the knowing subject is projected. Thus the conditional reality of the psycho-physical self can be likened to a shadow that, because it has a discernable presence, thinks of itself as an autonomous agent.

The close alliance of sapiential doctrine with human knowledge throughout the Middle Ages in Europe characterises those centuries as Europe's most metaphysical age. Yet even during this time the language of metaphysics and the language of theology were not clearly differentiated. Even here intellect was conceived in the mode of rational thought. The idea of intuition was coloured by the forms of empirical knowledge. In time this in itself permitted the emergence of the characteristically modern, humanist and materialist view of the creation,[10] a shift of perspective that eventually led to the supremacy of those modes of knowledge for which psycho-physical experience is the model. The collapse of Scholastic doctrine in the fourteenth century lent strength to the polarisation of thought towards human, as distinct from sapiential knowledge, eventually leading to the eclipse of the metaphysical perspective as the primary orientation of intelligence.

Although Scholasticism was directed towards the sapiential and metaphysical essence of man, its rationalist bias, by marginalising the intuitive 'ground' of knowledge, eventually neglected, as it were, to acknowledge its own non-discursive essence. This prepared the way for the assimilation of the spiritual discourse of theology to philosophical 'metaphysics'. What the dissolution of the Medieval cosmology permitted was

> the destruction of the idea of a qualitatively and ontologically differentiated world, and its replacement by that of an open, indefinite and even [quasi-] infinite universe, united and governed by the same [general] laws; a universe which, in contradiction to the traditional conception with its distinction . . . of the two worlds of Heaven and Earth, all things are on the same level of Being . . . The Laws of Heaven and the laws of Earth are merged together . . . And this implied the disappearance from the scientific outlook of all considerations based on value, on perfection, on harmony, on meaning and on purpose.[11]

Thus theology, philosophy, art, the sciences, gradually shorn of their qualitative and unifying cosmology, gained in independence and increasingly aligned themselves with a model of knowledge derived from empirical experience.

Thus, immediate 'reality' rather than the ultimately Real, by subtle degrees became the arbiter of artistic value, whether as the direct perception of phenomena in the visual arts, or as 'feeling' response in the auditory arts. Individual experience was to be the basis of all thought and action. Art was directed towards personal emotion. Henceforth, only the faculties of the psycho-physical self were to be called upon for their subjective response. Meaning, in the arts, began its descent towards gradually accepting only a psychic or phenomenal source as the causal 'energy' of all creating and perceiving.

This capitulation to a psycho-physical order of things eventually replaced the medieval conception of intellect as something divine that underwrites the arts by means of which man creates according to the laws of a paradigmatic model of supra-human inspiration. The divine nature of the intellect as knowing subject was essential to all medieval thought, which never forgot man's immortal destiny. St. Bonaventure, with an eye fixed on the ultimate goal of man, speaks of a divine rather than a 'psychic' faculty when he comments, in *Retracing the Arts to Theology*, that the purpose of the artificer is to make visible in his works that which is eternal and invisible so that all men might be lead through such creations to the Creator. He continues: 'If we consider the *effect* [of the artefact] we shall see therein the *pattern of human life* for every artificer, indeed, aims to produce work that is beautiful, useful, and enduring, and only when it possesses these three qualities is the work highly valued and acceptable.'[12]

For all that, medieval man still did not 'know' God except as a final cause. He was the supreme principle of a metaphysics that crystallised its approach to the Infinite in a logic that was refractory to its real mystery. Between the medieval, Christian view of God as the Creator of the world *ex nihilo*, and the eighteenth century view of Him as some huge mechanical inventor, a power appealed to to account for the creation of atoms there was no middle ground. The real spiritual need of man, how an understanding of God—the assimilation of the

Divine—can lead to a discernment of the Real and the illusory and an attachment to the Real, is side-tracked into the problem of how the intelligence can rationally account for the reality we call 'God'. None the less the medieval view was able to acknowledge a divine cause and a spiritual end for the contingencies of human thought and action. And it did permit a symbolic and contemplative view of nature interpreted in terms of substance, essence, matter, form, quality and quantity and not, as with the rationalist science of the seventeenth century, in terms of space, mass, energy and the like. As Seyyed Hossein Nasr has observed:

> The Middle Ages thus drew to a close in a climate in which the symbolic and contemplative view of nature had been for the most part replaced by a rationalistic view, and this in turn through the criticism of nominalist theologians had led to philosophical scepticism. Meanwhile, with the destruction of the gnostic and metaphysical elements within Christianity the cosmological sciences became opaque and incomprehensible and the cosmos itself was gradually secularized.[13]

The Renaissance began a development that subtly changed the symbolic and mythical expressions of metaphysical truth. If the Middle Ages accepted these modes of analogical discourse as the outward, tangible expression of a hidden, intangible reality, then the Renaissance reversed the process and instituted the study of myths, concentrating upon the problem of whether or not myths are objective, historical facts, and, if not, what their 'inventors' intended by them.

When we consider the thought and art of the new secularism, we discover in them an over-riding concern for 'self'-expression and 'self'-analysis. We witness the beginnings of the artist as a 'personality'—the historical perspective gains increasing validity. After The Divine Comedy the question of whether it is valid for a life or a work of art to represent an eternally present heavenly model or prototype was pushed to the margins of thought and artistic experience. Increasingly the artist strives to place his art in the context of profane history and secular values. And this characteristic becomes increasingly important for a viewpoint which, lacking a cosmology that validates the passage of time in terms of sacred history, is increasingly weighed down by the cumulative content of an ever evolving existential duration. Hence an escape from this burden is sought in elaborations of retrospective thought or abstract idealism. It is here that we find the nineteenth century hypostazisation of history prefigured. In the centuries before Dante a metaphysical viewpoint made of this life a preparation for the life beyond. A need to escape into the past would only have been conceivable in terms of a return to the paradigmatic 'Golden Age'. Although the thought and art of the two centuries that followed Dante did not see man as a completely autonomous being or deny the gift of Grace there is little doubt that it was the *sensational*[14] nature of the individual human spirit that was its central motif.

The Renaissance was the beginning of the discovery that the world need not be considered a mirror of a celestial reality, and that man might be considered in existential isolation from the Divine. And since this entails the beginning of the abolition of even human values, God in turns becomes merely a principle of a theoretical metaphysics —as He is in Descartes where, once he is 'proven', He is best forgotten. But more than anything else is incurred the loss within every intellectual discipline, of that sapiential dimension upon which all knowledge depends, and by means of which the mind has its hold upon the qualitative essences of things. In myth, symbol and in art generally, metaphysical truths become opaque to the intelligence. The great delight of the Renaissance intellectuals was to study the ancients as *allegory*. The studies of Gombrich, Wind, Panovsky and Seznec demonstrate that, because of the increasing validity of the historical perspective, the Renaissance artists and poets looked back to the Greek and Roman mysteries to allegorise them into morality figures. Thus the symbolism of the Middle Ages, having lost its contemplative basis, begun to *veil* rather than *reveal*.

Inasmuch as modern man is heir to the Renaissance, so he is the victim of these metaphysical transpositions effected during the all-important years between 1400 and 1600. It may be that philosophy in the West is still prepared to postulate to the rational intelligence that there remains a portion of man's being that transcends both time and space; but that man is made *in the image of God*, in the milieu of the arts, is now a proposition rarely defended. The sapiential doctrines of the sacred traditions none the less are founded upon just this principle: that there is in man an immortal Spirit and a mortal soul and the immortal Spirit is the *essence* of every being as well as its ultimate *end*. The Renaissance and every humanist development since have seen to it that man remains subject both to a nature opaque to his thought and to truths contingent upon merely personal experience. It is more than possible to argue that thought and art since the beginning of the Renaissance have 'descended' through the hierarchy of the faculties so that today all they demand is a mere passive ideation or *sensation*. The loss of objective criteria implicit in such a descent limits the intelligence to merely subjective truth or falsity, seeing that it is the hopeless prisoner of a 'self'-willed autonomy. In this measure the modern mind can be likened to a man of partial sight staring into a shattered mirror.

NOTES

1. For an exposition of the meaning of metaphysics from a universal perspective see René Guénon, 'Oriental Metaphysics', in *The Sword of Gnosis*, edited by Jacob Needleman, (Baltimore, 1974), pp.40–56. In this essay Guénon gives his reasons for the use of the singular 'metaphysic'. The present chapter is indebted to Guénon's exposition.

2. René Guénon, *East and West*, translated by William Massey, (London, 1941), p.57–8.

3. See chapter 19, 'Man and Certainty' in *Logic and Transcendence* by Frithjof Schuon, translated by Peter N. Townsend (N.Y., 1975).

4. A. K. Coomaraswamy, 'On the Pertinence of Philosophy' in *What is Civilisation?* (Ipswich, 1989), p. 15.

5. René Guénon, 'Oriental Metaphysics' op. cit. p. 44.

6. René Guénon, *Introduction to the Study of the Hindu Doctrines*, translated by Marco Pallis (London, 1945), p. 117.

7. Aristotle's is only one such formulation; the Scholastic definition of art as a 'virtue of the practical intelligence' would do equally as well.

8. Mircea Eliade, *The Myth of the Eternal Return*, translated by William R. Trask (N.Y., 1954), pp. 3–4.

9. Eliade, Op. cit. p. 34.

10. One should add that the modern age is no longer 'humanist' in the Renaissance sense but continues to show every sign of an increasing de-humanisation—the logical end of the humanist view?

11. Alexandre Koyré, *Metaphysics and Measurement*, (London, 1968) p. 20. It is necessary to change 'universal' to 'general' in this passage since what the author has in mind is a knowledge accessible to the discursive faculty which itself is closed to all that is truly universal. Such 'laws' pertain to the individual order of manifestation. As Guénon has pointed out, it is important to distinguish the universal from the general, thereby saving endless confusion, seeing that the terms have become interchangeable in modern speech. The 'universal' is not a summation or collectivity of all particular things, any more than the infinite is an indefinite summation of the finite, or eternity the indefinite extension of time. And this accounts also for the addition of quasi.

12. The translation of Bonaventure, *De Reductione Artium ad Theologiam*, is that of Sister Emma Thérèse Healy, (Saint Bonaventure, N.Y., 1955). With the Renaissance the beautiful and the useful are seldom thereafter to form a unity in the West.

13. S. H. Nasr, *The Encounter of Man and Nature*, (London, 1969), pp. 63–4.

14. 'Sensation is very frequently identified so closely with Self that it is held to be the deepest level of man's being. In the western world it so happens that feeling is more usually identified with the Self than any other faculty, for which cause the feeling element in religion—moral value, ecstasy, consolation—is apt to be regarded, not as analogy of the ultimate Reality, but as its very essence. This predominance of what Guénon terms the "sentimental" element in religion gives the modern Christian a standpoint from which metaphysics seems cold, amoral, and impersonal, if not absolutely meaningless.' A. W. Watts, *The Supreme Identity* (London, 1950), p. 73.

Tradition and the Individual

THE IDEA OF TRADITION HAS LONG PREOCCUPIED THE modern mind. No doubt the sense of its loss as well as the realisation of its importance for the ordering and orientation of human affairs are the cause of this concern. This being said, however, tradition is seldom understood in its primal sense. In the *anti*-traditional milieu that is the modern world, the word is misused in ways both deliberate and unconscious. The word 'tradition' is now likely to figure in the dismissal of any custom or practise whose meaning is no longer understood, or in conjunction with any matter that is deemed to be out of date and irrelevant to modern interests. In fact, the modern mind is founded upon a relentlessly progressive stance according to which tradition is more or less thought of as the corpse of the past and is best disposed of, the sooner the better.

But for all that the modern mind cannot relinquish entirely the idea of tradition and has at times taken some pains to distinguish and define it. Of equal importance has been the problem—one might say the anxiety—of establishing a true relationship between tradition and the individual. This relationship necessarily accompanies the idea of tradition since it is one of the primary functions of a tradition, in relation to culture, to unite in a common principle that which would otherwise appear to be an unending stream of unrelated ideas and events.

During the early part of this century a number of writers whose views on tradition were subsequently to prove influential tackled the subject in books and essays. Perhaps the best known of these was T. S. Eliot's essay 'Tradition and the Individual Talent', in which he seemed to many to have established the terms and extent of the subject from the modern point of view. Far less widely known was the more profound notion of tradition formulated by René Guénon, A. K. Coomaraswamy,

Frithjof Schuon and others. Whereas Eliot's notion of tradition was drawn up on the basis of European culture, the idea of tradition that we find in the works of Guénon and his associates is founded on the universal, metaphysical principles that have been the perennial bedrock of the world's religions. We will return later to Eliot's more familiar ideas. For the moment let us take a closer look at this perennial notion of tradition and its relationship with history and the individual.

The word 'tradition', like many other words one can offer as examples of extreme semantic depreciation in contemporary usage, being allowed to mean almost anything inevitably comes to mean almost nothing.[1] The difficulty is here compounded simply because the concept of tradition contains a superabundant richness of connotations such as to make neatness of definition, even if it were desirable, near to impossible. It is the same with tradition as with all things whose origin needs to be traced back to Revelation. The problem remains one of grasping the ontological mystery of the passage from essence to manifestation—from beyond the realm of time and space to the world of continuous generation and decay.

The word 'tradition' (from the Greek *paradidomi*, Latin *traditio*) indicates a transmission, a handling over, a handing down of something. Clearly this transmission must involve some sort of language, whether written or pronounced. The *what* and the *how* of this transmission comprise the two primary aspects of tradition. The *content* of tradition implies a vertical axis of descent as to its transhuman and integrative principle while its *modus operandi* implies a horizontal chain of transmission whose continuity is other than the historical process of change itself. It is important not to confuse the content and transmission of tradition with the temporal succession of history, since to do so is to impoverish the very means by which man is attached to the sacred.

Indeed, both content and transmission must remain attached to their transcendent principle if tradition is to be saved from an 'evolution' in which it becomes something other than what is potential to it 'in the beginning'. Being a form of initiation, a tradition must be transmitted in conformity with the integral meaning and possibility of the principle it expresses and from which it derives its being (Christian *Love*; Moslem *Unity*; Buddhist *Self*). Assuredly a tradition can 'develop', for it is a living thing, but such development is always an extension and an application of its principle as opposed to its assimilation to any purely historical process. Any such assimilation can result in the weakening of the ontological links that bind a tradition to its reflection in a civilisation and a culture, since in the very act of transmission there remains the possibility of dissolution and involvement with profane knowledge and conceptions.

Tradition, then, is far from being an accumulation of human endeavour and fabrication even if it does have a history. Even if we grant that the embodiment of a tradition in a civilisation is coloured and conditioned by the characteristics of a particular historical period, none the less we have to recognise that the atemporal, supra-formal principle of a tradition, that which gives it its power to unite in a common understanding the diversity of what is scattered throughout time and place, is proof enough that a tradition, though it is *in* time, is not *of* it. Which is to say a tradition has both a transcendent and an immanent aspect. It is in virtue of its Divine principle that attachment to and immersion in a tradition becomes a mode of internal witness which provides the objectification that lifts the human subject clear of what would otherwise be a meaningless succession of historical events, and from which no individual could otherwise ever hope to extricate himself. Insofar as man makes 'sense' of history, or strives to do so, he depends upon the effective reality of this supra-formal principle to save himself from being engulfed by the determinism that is the relentless flow of actions and events. It is the realisation of this internal witness which preserves that Truth, the knowledge of which 'will make you free' (John 8:32), and which reveals the atemporal criteria by which temporal movement can be measured.

To understand tradition as meaning simply the continuity of history comes about as the result of an error that could hardly be made were it not for the prevailing conception of man as being, to all intents and purposes an autonomous, soulless being trapped in an existential isolation that acknowledges only the dualistic claims of mind against matter. This post-Cartesian conception discards outright the soul as the active organ of spiritual perception. Its proper role denied, what hope is there that the soul can act as the ever-present witness to those internal qualities that elude the funeral cortège of time? He who seeks possession of a living tradition understands the need to free himself from the illusion that the 'archives' of the past represents the vital substance of a tradition. For him the regeneration of the soul alone permits in turn the renewal of a tradition. It is in the soul, that the association of a tradition with change escapes the impotence of being interpreted exclusively in terms of all that man himself has contributed to the wreckage of historical time. Otherwise there could be no possibility of spiritual renewal, only the sterility and the deception of the customary and the commonplace. Only in the subtle ontology of its integral perceptions can the soul recognise those qualitative essences whose forms cheat that inner death that insists that past experience can never be freed from what made it the past.

All of which presupposes that there is no such thing as a profane tradition. Profanity is the desacralisation of tradition. There is no tradition apart from the Divine and its earthly reverberations; Tradition as such. And this latter is not a sort of amalgam and summation of all the differing traditions that have been revealed to man, completing and perfecting them in a way each of them is incapable of doing on its own. Insofar as man has access to the Divine he does so by way of a tradition; that is, he is immersed in ways of being and doing that have been determined by a spiritual principle addressed to that portion of mankind it is his destiny to belong to. In other words, he cannot hear the 'music' of Tradition as such apart from the 'performance' of a tradition.

To say that tradition must be rigorously dissociated from all that threatens to lose it among the contents of history, is another way of saying that a tradition must be capable of preserving for us the objective norm by which we can know who we are apart from that which merely happens to us. Despite whatever clues may be offered by thoughts, actions and reactions to external events, to seek to define man purely in terms of his thinking and his acting will impoverish the human self-image because such a definition must shelve the question of the ultimate nature of the subject who thinks and acts.[2] Just as appearances are logically *of* something that is 'hidden', so the ultimate selfhood of the person is 'masked' by the protean abundance of his or her thoughts and actions. It is the indistinct subject that gives coherence to the psycho-physical existence of the individual, a subject that can obviously never become an object of knowledge so far as the individual knowing subject is concerned. The individual subject can be understood in this light to possess a defining essence that is never simply the cumulative body of psycho-physical states which are in reality so many modes of the hidden subject. The existence of the indistinct subject allows us to speak of man as being able to know, in any objective sense, Truth, the divine immanence at the root of consciousness. It is essentially the purpose of tradition to safeguard the divine immanence of consciousness, as it is formally the purpose of tradition to participate the transcendent dimension of truth throughout human thought and action. Vladimir Lossky states the case precisely:

> Tradition is the *unique mode* of receiving [the Truth]. We say specifically *unique mode* and not *uniform mode*, for to Tradition in its pure notion there belongs nothing formal. It does not impose on human consciousness formal guarantees of the truths of faith, but gives access to the discovery of their inner evidence. It is not the content of Revelation, but the light that reveals it; it is not the word, but the living breath which makes the words heard at the same time as the silence from which it came; it is not the Truth, but a communication of the Spirit of Truth outside which the Truth cannot be received.[3]

It becomes clear that tradition presupposes the spiritual nature of intelligence, and stands over and against the dissipating forces of spiritual, moral and artistic improvisation for their own sake. As a mode of spiritual inheritance and cultural preservation, tradition stands guard over the coherence and the integrity of inspiration, thought and action by means of ritual action, mythical thought patterns and archetypal forms of symbolic expression. Thus it aligns man with the reverberations of the Spirit in the human soul, and which await actualisation in some form by means of the individual's inborn gifts.

Tradition, then, is the intrinsic mode of a specific body of revealed knowledge, and as such is the integral ontological light by which what is potential to the Divine is realised in human consciousness. Like all metaphysical knowledge, tradition takes account of the inexpressible, the silence that makes possible the word, the void that makes possible all manifestation. Tradition permits intelligence to hold a mirror to the Infinite in order to recognise—in accordance with cosmic principles—its affinity with it. Which is why tradition cannot be impoverished or fabricated from merely human means since it is only by the light of tradition that man is able to understand the ultimate truth of his subjective nature, a nature whose limitations, in terms of that light, are a state of unknowingness that cannot, be mere recourse to itself, overcome its own ignorance.

Inasmuch as a tradition is that light 'outside which the Truth cannot be received', it represents a perspective by which the human subject may see beyond those very conditions and limitations that make him the individual he is. It implies immutable criteria not only with respect to intelligence but to the objectivity of the knowing subject's ultimate knowledge as well. It may be that nothing is known except in the mode of the knower, but there can be no certainty as to the objective truth of the knower's knowledge of himself unless a distinction is possible between Intellect as such and its reflection in the individual mind. To lump together discursive thought, intuition and imagination as faculties of a vaguely defined 'mind', and then to suppose that the operations of this 'mind' have their sources entirely within individual subjective consciousness, is to degrade and diminish both Truth and intelligence.

As Frithjof Schuon has pointed out, this subjective hypothesis harbours a fundamental inconsistency:

> That man can never pass beyond what is 'subjective' and human is the most gratuitous and contradictory of hypotheses. Who then defines 'human subjectivity' as such? If it is human subjectivity itself which does so, then there is no such thing as objective knowledge and no definition is possible; if something other than this subjectivity does so, then it is clearly wrong to say that man cannot pass beyond it. It is clear that no definition has value apart from its objectivity, that is to say apart from absence of error; on the other hand one cannot seek to enclose the Universe in the 'subjective and human' while at the same time admitting of a point of view beyond this same subjectivity which can consequently define it.

By the same token it is clear that human subjectivity as such can no more be said to think for itself than one can say that an eye can see vision. For, as Schuon continues,

> If it is a man who defines himself, what objective value can be attached to this definition? And, if there is no objective value, no transcendent criterion, why think? If it is enough to be a man in order to be in the right, why seek to refute human errors?[4]

If the objective status of Truth and its proper relationship to the human subject is to be maintained, then the apparent subjectivity of all modes of individual thought must be seen as projected upon a consciousness without individuality and without plurality, namely, the Divine Intellect, which intelligence reflects and embodies. In every effort of individual communication a consciousness without plurality is by definition invoked. All the sacred traditions teach how the many individual dispositions of mind are in essence consubstantial with the supra-human Intellect that transcends the 'separateness' of individual minds and provides the true and ultimate ground of an understanding *in common.*

T. S. Eliot certainly expressed the standpoint of the modern mind, with its characteristic sense of its own religious disorientation, when he wrote in 'Tradition and the Individual Talent'; '. . . tradition cannot be inherited, and if you want it you must obtain it by great labour'. In stressing the great labour that the acquisition of tradition requires, Eliot in part echoes the view of W. B. Yeats (in *The Celtic Twilight*), who none the less approached the matter from a very different perspective:

> In a society that has cast out imaginative tradition, only a few people —three or four thousand out of millions—favoured by their own characters and by happier circumstances, and only then after much labour, have understanding of imaginative things, and yet 'the imagination is the man himself'.5

The idea that one has to labour in order to possess tradition is itself symptomatic of modern man's spiritual disorientation. Within the matrix of a society in which the institutions, rituals and social structures are themselves the embodiment and expression of metaphysical truth, man has no more to labour to understand tradition than the fish has to labour to 'understand' water. Tradition is simply the natural element in which he has his being.

In an important sense, however, Yeats's understanding is the inverse of Eliot's. For Yeats, tradition is immanent and fundamental to man's nature. For Eliot—who thought that tradition 'cannot be inherited', despite his claim that it 'involves . . . the historical sense . . . which is a sense of the timeless as well as the temporal'—tradition is external to man, something added to his effort to produce a culture and which has its roots in the notion of the contemporaneous value of man's cultural 'successes' (Eliot's word). It is really a view dominated by time, and insofar as it implicitly formulates a philosophy of human intelligence, it attempts to trace the relationship between tradition and the individual mind from past phases of man's cultural history. Indeed, on the basis of this derivation, Eliot went on to develop his theory of creative depersonalisation, with its agent the 'objective correlative'.

In all this the spiritual roots of tradition are obscured and impoverished. Man cannot arrive at criteria of immutable value on the basis of anything so vague as a sense of the contemporary relevance of bits and pieces of his own created past. By what trans-cultural principle is such a sense to be ordered? What man *does* can only be valued in the light of what man *is*—which points to the need, in all cultural activity, to take into account the non-discursive essence of the intelligence and the uncreated essence of the individual being.

Doubtless 'Tradition and the Individual Talent' does not represent Eliot's most mature reflections on the subject, but we are here concerned primarily with its important and widespread influence. Even when he came to reconsider the essay, as he did in *After Strange Gods* (1934), he could only redefine tradition as 'rather a way of feeling and acting which characterises a group throughout generations; and that it must be, or that many of the elements in it must be, unconscious'. In such a definition the question of the supra-human source of tradition is put aside so that all criteria of objectivity and permanence guaranteed by that source come to seem determined by the contingencies of human experience.[6] With his insistence that it involves the 'historical sense', and by his inclination to see tradition as belonging in some way to 'cultural success' Eliot unavoidably adulterates the notion of tradition. In his view the appeal of tradition is not to those metaphysical principles that are the ever-abundant source of eternal reality and wisdom, but to such externalities of human effort as shape the world of cultural history.

On Eliot's terms it is evidently not a question of the degree to which metaphysical principles are ever-present realities of knowing and being. What is absent from his formulation is that genuine interior bond by which the archetypal reality draws back to itself, through the experience of the individual, what is originally intrinsic to it.

The limitations of Eliot's conclusions were perhaps predetermined;

firstly, by his concern to define the nature and place of tradition from within the confines of a particular perspective of modern European thought; and secondly, and more importantly, by an intellectual stand-point whose foundations rested on the post-Renaissance 'humanist' culture rooted in post-Cartesian dualism. The underlying assumptions of his formulation were shaped by a history and a culture whose understanding of the terms 'truth', 'reality', 'knowledge', as well as its tacit human self-image, were themselves *anti*-traditional. The history and the culture on which he implicitly draws are characterised by their deviation from those metaphysical and spiritual norms whose effective existence attaches the individual to the divine reality. At least at the time of writing his essay, Eliot precluded the possibility of such an attachment, for his formulation of tradition, as he admitted, halted 'at the frontier of metaphysics'. At which point the poet had arrived at the threshold of tradition.

Against the earlier view of Eliot the critic we must balance the more comprehensive and later view of Eliot the poet.[7] Because his earlier poems are so readily valued for their 'modernity' and 'originality', the deeper achievement of his later poetry is sometimes overlooked. In an age that has succumbed to the superstition of 'thinking for oneself' the apparent freedom of a trackless desert must seem preferable to following a path that is overgrown through neglect. One can only suppose this to be the premiss of those who regard Eliot's retreat to the Church and his 'falling back' upon religion as a sign of weakness. It surely is the case that Eliot discovered in his maturity that the way to the truth had been trodden by countless generations throughout history and yet is not to be found *in* history.

We can certainly point to the poetry as reflecting the gradual development of its author's understanding of the relationship between tradition as a unique mode of truth and the individual consciousness. The shift of emphasis can be traced from the nightmarish autonomy of Prufrock's post-Cartesian psychic world, through the ambivalent subjectivity of Tiresias who

> throbbing between two lives,
> Old man with wrinkled female breasts

'sees all' and 'foresuffers all', who is thus no character yet unites all the other characters of *The Waste Land*, to the universal consciousness enunciated in Heraclitus' 'Although the Logos is common the many live as though they had private understanding' (which forms an epigraph to 'Burnt Norton' and the implications of which are a recurring theme in *Four Quartets*).

The illusion of individual autonomy that each 'self'-experience creates consists precisely in limiting subjective intelligence to operating exclusively within the continuum of events in the space-time world. In the impotence of Prufrock we can discern the morbid dilemma of the 'thinking individual' who, on the basis of a private psycho-mental awareness, is locked in the passive, self-enclosed network of thoughts that places his identity at the mercy of their own evermore reflexive and attenuated inter-relationships:

> Do I dare
> Disturb the Universe?
> In a minute there is time
> For decisions and revisions which a minute will reverse

Only tradition in its primal sense can provide the transcendent dimension whereby the seemingly independent reality of the isolated 'I' is both recognised and vanquished, for only in that 'unique mode' of intelligence safeguarded by tradition can there be found the means of discernment to objectify the human subject and so bind it back to that innate principle which itself links man to all that is above subjectivity as such. Only in such a context is the passage away from private and habitual experience illuminated, and the limitations that psycho-physical awareness imposes upon the mind overcome. As Eliot acknowledges in 'The Dry Salvages':

Men's curiosity searches past and future
And clings to that dimension. But to apprehend
The point of intersection of the timeless
With time, is an occupation for the saint—
No occupation either, but something given
And taken, in a lifetime's death in Love,
Ardour and selflessness and self-surrender.

More concerned with elaborating knowledge than with wisdom, with mental concepts than with metaphysical discernment, with intellectual sophistication rather than with truth, that 'searching curiosity' that Eliot speaks of, which absorbs the mind into the mirrored surface of its own protean experience at the same time obscures the uncreated essence of the Intellect upon which, like a screen, all knowledge and experience are projected. In 'East Coker' Eliot acknowledged,

There is, it seems to us,
At best, only a limited value
In the knowledge derived from experience.
The knowledge imposes a pattern, and falsifies,
For the pattern is new in every moment
And every moment is a new and shocking
Valuation of all we have been.

When the content of that 'knowledge derived from experience' is studied for what it can be made to yield on its own terms, it is as if, mesmerised by its own subjective prolongations, the mind is too bemused ever to question the objective status of that which occupies it. In the sapiential context of tradition, however, the divine ground of consciousness is admitted at the outset as the *modus operandi* of all intellectualization and its actualisation taken for granted as the necessary condition of objective knowledge.

There is a need, then, to acknowledge that the ultimate referent of the subject, like an indistinct dimension, stands apart from its reflection in discursive thought, an identity made manifest in the humility of recognising the infinite and common essence of all being, as Eliot likewise acknowledges in the same poem:

> The only wisdom we can hope to acquire
> Is the wisdom of humility: humility is endless.

For the action of humility destroys at the roots all those notions derived from subjective 'thinking', whose web is so cunningly woven in the postulation of its own self-centred reality. Humility attacks the illusory identification of the knowing subject with subjectivity itself, for only in the plenitude of the moment when the Knower is the sole object of all knowledge is the only possible wisdom achieved—the chasm between knowing and being finally bridged. Again, from Eliot's 'East Coker':

> In order to arrive there,
> To arrive where you are, to get from where you are not,
>   You must go by a way wherein there is no ecstasy.
> In order to arrive at what you do not know
>   You must go by a way which is the way of ignorance.
> In order to possess what you do not possess
>   You must go by way of dispossession.
> In order to arrive at what you are not
>   You must go through the way in which you are not.
> And what you do not know is the only thing you know
> And what you own is what you do not own
> And where you are is where you are not.

In the uncreated essence of all subjectivity is the sole objective end: 'In my beginning is my end'.

So we conclude that the importance of Eliot's views on tradition are to be found not in their formulation in his earlier critical writings but as they are expressed later in his *Four Quartets*. Here they are at their most profound and mature. Indeed, here, as near as ever he did, the poet implicitly declares himself an *anti*-modernist.

It is the earthly destiny of man to return from whence he came—God. As Frithjof Schuon has observed: 'The substance of human knowledge is Knowledge of the divine Substance'. On the evidence of the cultures of the sacred traditions we find every indication we could want to confirm the universality of the link between human history and the plane of divine energies whose imprint, by means of the eternal archetypes, determines the norms of cultural meanings and values. Everywhere we look in traditional cultures we see the spiritual adventures of man, those preludic journeys that prepare him for the life beyond the particular 'time' and 'place' of his earthly existence. Everywhere there is the constant attempt, founded upon spiritual knowledge, to understand the phenomenal world's transparency in relation to its divine source. For traditional man everywhere the generated world is instinct with the sacred reality of the Spirit. For him, as Blake wrote, 'Eternity is in love with the production of time'. As with all things of a spiritual nature it comes down to the state of preparedness of the individual, for 'nothing is known except in the mode of the knower'. This 'mode of the knower' involves more than merely subjective experience, for such experiences would be nothing were it not for the objective status of the intellect. Discursive intelligence, mirroring and 'making sense' of phenomenal reality, has need of a point of reference beyond that reality in order to set the seal of meaning on what it discovers. The ultimate as well as logical context for an understanding of the world of time and space is one in which their origin beyond time and space is taken into account. Time can have no beginning *in* time; space no extensive reality *from* space itself. If we believe that the reality that lies beyond the world of empirical experience is unknowable, which we do, if only unwittingly, in taking an exclusively quantifiable view of things, then the intelligence must abandon what appears at all times to be its immediate and ultimate objective: to 'take in' that which *is* in order to distinguish the Real from the illusory, truth from falsehood.

NOTES

1. Of the word 'myth', for example, we have at the one extreme Coomaraswamy's 'myth embodies the nearest approach to absolute truth that can be stated in words', and at the other the *Shorter Oxford Dictionary*'s 'a purely fictitious narrative': this last eliciting from David Jones, 'a bloody lie in fact . . . that is about the limit in loss of meaning'. Elsewhere, with his characteristic eye to the incarnational quality of history, he glosses the word as follows: 'To conserve, to develop, to bring together, to make significant for the present what the past holds, without dilution or any deleting, but rather by understanding and transubstantiating the material, this is the function of genuine myth, neither pedantic nor popularising, not indifferent to scholarship, nor antiquarian, but saying always: "of those thou has given me have I lost none".' (John 17:12) *Epoch and Artist* (London, 1959), p. 243.

2. For a discussion of the principal dangers and delusions of self-knowledge from the perspective of a tradition—in this case the Sufi tradition of Islam—see William Chittick, *Sufism, a short introduction* (Oxford, 2000), Chapter 4, 'Self-Help'.

3. Vladimir Lossky, *In the Image of Likeness of God* (London, 1975), pp. 151–52.

4. Frithjof Schuon, *Spiritual Perspectives and Human Facts*, trans. by Macleod Matheson (London, 1954), pp. 16–17.

5. *Mythologies* (London, 1932), pp. 14.

6. This illustrates the inversion of values, so prevalent in modern thought, whereby explanation proceeds from 'below upward' instead of 'above downwards'. See René Guénon, *The Reign of Quantity and the Signs of the Times*, translated by Lord Northbourne (London, 1953), Chapters I and II.

7. Eliot was later to study Sanscrit and comparative religion as well as confessing to the influence of A. K. Coomaraswamy and Frithjof Schuon.

Minding True Things

Let us, ciphers . . . on your imaginary forces work . . .
Piece out your imperfections with your thoughts . . . and
make imaginary puissance . . . work, work your thoughts
 . . . yet sit and see, minding true things by what their
mock'ries be.

Prologue, *King Henry the Fifth*

SHAKESPEARE'S CONFIDENT APPEAL TO HIS AUDIENCE WAS
likely met. But what poet now could make such an appeal, suggesting
that in the forms imagination takes we have the key to the Real and the
True? For the modern mind imagination gives access to the untrue, the
fictional. Of little epistemological interest to philosophy and seldom
dealt with to any effect by writers on the arts, imagination has now a
neglected status that befits its role as agent of the unreal.

Put at its simplest, imagination is the faculty of producing images in
the mind. In addition, the imaginative image is an intermediary in two
senses: between the inner and the outer and between the sensory and
the intelligible. Imagination thus provides the intellect with what Jean
Borella has called a 'substitute matter' which acts as the objective basis
for thought to accomplish its activity. But what status do imaginative
images have? Where are they to be located in relation to the Real?

Henry Corbin has several times in his work drawn attention to
the fact that the 'official knowledge' taught in our time always leads
back to sense-perception or to general laws abstracted from empirical knowledge. What might be said to be in between is thought of as
'imaginary'—unreal. To enquire into the ontological status of the
imagination in our time is to do so against a predisposition of the
modern mind to accept the primary concepts of truth and reality as

having been subordinated to a certain worldview. Having turned away from contemplation of the Eternal and the Absolute, the modern mind seeks to establish truth in the domain of man's interaction with the relative and the contingent. Our enquiry arises from within the framework of a type of knowledge that no longer views man as a microcosm possessing inherent spiritual possibilities whose realization depends upon just such a contemplation. So far as the modern mind is concerned, 'knowledge' is that which aims to satisfy a need to explain in rational terms, the nature and function of empirical experience. Even though the ultimate value of this type of knowledge is occasionally questioned, it remains the case that the modern mind is predisposed to think of reality as being a substance outside of mind.

We may look to an historical cause by way of at least a partial explanation of why this is so. It is the extent to which the modern mind has inherited its mental disposition from the mind/matter dualism formulated by Descartes, but latent in certain aspects of post-medieval thought and beyond. We cannot doubt that the Cartesian formula underscores what Gilbert Durand has called the great 'schizomorphic' structure of western intelligence whereby there is a disconnection between the 'I' and the world: *res cogitans* against *res extensa*; that is, thinking as an activity ranged against the otherness of external things. So far as 'official knowledge' is concerned, such a dualism has been to all intents and purposes the basis of the empirical sciences whose elaboration has determined the quantitative, materialist 'topography' of reality for the modern mind.

In speaking of a decline of imagination we have in mind the fact that the historical development of the rationalist dilemma has impoverished imaginative thought to the point where it is no longer considered as the distinct organ of *active* spiritual perception of the soul. If the modern mind has any conception of imagination at all it is either, on the one hand, a process of forming images in the mind after an event in sensory experience or, on the other, as phantasy—an 'invented' image indirectly derived from appearances in the world of sense. In either case imagination is left to reconstitute external events and

44

appearances in the mind, but at the same mental level at which the mind finds itself trapped by the terms of a mind/matter dichotomy it might have supposed imagination would surmount: the disjunctive worlds of on the one hand the private 'I' and on the other a reality external to it. Hence it comes about that the content of imaginative experience is merely the 'fiction' of private experience. There could hardly be a more withering dismissal of anything we are not inclined to regard as being in the least real than to say of it 'you must be imagining things!' That imagination should be limited to these notional aspects of its function is due to the dualism of thinking divorced from being, itself a consequence of the erosion of the traditional anthropological triad of body, soul and spirit.

Imagination can have no active spiritual role other than by being situated within a cosmology and an anthropology that admits to a hierarchy of degrees of being. When a materialist philosophy, in effect, reduces everything to a single level of reality, it is to be expected that intelligence itself will be blind to the metaphysical necessity of there being a domain of forms that correspond to each of the primary levels of the microcosmic, triadic structure. That is: the material forms of the corporeal world corresponding to sense perception; the world of intelligible essences beyond formal manifestation, corresponding to the highest intuition of intellect; and the intermediate world of archetypal forms (and, according to the visionary mystics and divinely inspired poets, the world of angels and spirits) linking the lower and higher worlds.

By means of a knowledge that is cosmological in scope and analogical in operation the transmutation of the sensible world into its spiritual *meaning* takes place. By the forms of the intermediate world of the soul's imaginative perception, whose forms are less immaterial than those of the intelligible realm and more immaterial than those of the corporeal world, we re-cognise the manner in which the highest can be symbolised by what is qualitatively beneath it.

But the rehabilitation of imagination as an active spiritual function could not come about by simply giving thought to it as just another problem of philosophy that seeks an acceptable formulation. Certain metaphysical conditions must effectively operate if imaginative cognition is to be spiritually valid. In the first place and as a minimum requirement, it is necessary to restore, through contemplation and prayer, the ambience of intellectual intuition itself in order to bridge the chasm that divides being from knowing. Without this spiritual ambience imaginative experience has no access to the level of reference that corresponds to the soul's act of perception. To be spiritually valid imagination must safeguard against the arbitrary improvisations of purely subjective phantasy. In drawing the soul away from its attachment to sensory perception, true imaginative experience must polarise perception in accordance with values and meanings derived from celestial levels of reference. This is exactly what Blake refers to in his famous description of Imagination in *A Vision of the Last Judgment*:

> This world of Imagination is the world of Eternity; it is the divine bosom into which we shall all go after the death of the Vegetated body. This World of Imagination is Infinite & Eternal, whereas the world of Generation, or Vegetation, is Finite & Temporal. There Exists in that Eternal World the Permanent Realities of Every Thing which we see reflected in this Vegetable Glass of Nature. All things are comprehended in their Eternal Forms in the divine body of the Saviour, the True Vine of Eternity, The Human Imagination, who appear'd to Me as Coming to Judgment among his Saints & throwing off the Temporal that the Eternal might be Establish'd.

In this traditional conception imaginative intuition is akin to visionary consciousness that not only guarantees the metaphysical status of the *mode* of perception but also guarantees the ontological objectivity of *what* is perceived. Corbin, from his studies of many Sufi spiritual masters, confirms Blake's experience:

> This approach to imagination, which has always been of prime importance for our mystical theosophers, provided them with a

basis for demonstrating the validity of dreams and of the visionary reports describing and relating 'events in Heaven' as well as the validity of symbolic rites. It offered proof of the reality of the places that occur during intense meditation, the validity of inspired imaginative vision, of cosmogonies and theogonies and above all the veracity of the *spiritual* meaning perceived in the imaginative information supplied by prophetic revelations.[1]

The spiritual act of imagination takes place in a subtle domain of forms whose symbolic, transmutational power enables it to avoid squandering its powers in an effort to construct a unity of *res extensa* according to the mode of *res cogitans*. This is not to imply that imagination seeks to *devalue* the world of sensory perception. On the contrary, true imaginative experience seeks to apprehend ('join together'—symbolise 'with each other'—from the Greek verb *symballien*) every level of manifestation as it subsists in the perfection of Being itself—an apprehension by which to *know* and to *be* are consubstantial realities.[2]

In the perception of the domain of celestial spirits; in their living embodiment in myth and rite; in the celebration in song, dance, epic and the initiatic crafts, is preserved and strengthened the 'organic' framework in which the world of nature and the domain of imaginative experience correspond, shaping man's existential experience to the true rhythm of the Eternal. The very dislocation of spiritual from psychological, psychological from empirical experience that characterises modern man's agnostic disposition may be directly attributed to the withdrawal of that subtle world whose imaginative status occupies such an important part of the traditional cosmologies. As Corbin has warned, the magnitude of the loss 'becomes apparent when we consider that this intermediate world is the realm where the conflict which split the Occident, the conflict between theology and philosophy, between faith and knowledge, between symbol and history, is resolved.'

Significantly, it fell to a poet, Shelley, to prophetically and tragically note the consequences that, 'for want of correspondence with those first principles which belong to imagination, wrought effects which must ever flow from an unmitigated exercise of the calculating faculty'. In his *Defence of Poetry* of 1821 he had found it necessary to affirm among 'reasoners and mechanists' the traditional doctrine of imagination— one that, as he described it, acts in its perceptions 'in a divine and unapprehended manner, beyond and above consciousness'. Now that we are heirs to the collapse of all but the minimum of cultural and social institutions, it is relevant to note Shelley's sure instinct in observing the repercussions that follow from the withdrawal of metaphysical intuition: 'The end of social corruption is to destroy all sensibility to pleasure; . . . . It begins at imagination and the intellect as at the core, and distributes itself thence as a paralysing venom, through the affections into the very appetites until all becomes a torpid mass in which hardly sense survives.'

The primary analogy relating to imagination that is always the pivotal point of the traditional doctrines is that of cosmic with human creation. Indeed in the idea of *creatio ex nihilo* we meet with a conception of the Godhead who by the power of *Creative Imagination* (Emanation) brings the world into being from the potencies latent in His Essence.[3] It is in imitation of this act that the human artist gives form to (objectivises) what he first of all conceives within as a possibility inherent in his being.

Such a doctrine does not appear to be far from Coleridge's famous definition, in his *Biographia Literaria*, of 'primary Imagination' as 'the living Power and prime Agent of all human perception, and as a repetition in the finite mind of the external act of creation in the infinite I AM'. This definition, we recall, arose from Coleridge's concern to distinguish between 'fancy and Imagination' which had, in contemporary usage, become as 'two names with the one meaning, or, at furthest, the lower and higher degree of one and the same power'. But in seeing in imagination a 'dim Analogue of Creation' Coleridge gave it the emphasis of an organic process whose 'rules . . . are themselves the very powers of growth and production'. In this we can sense a foreshadowing of that method whereby the European mind, its interest in transcendent truth all but gone, was gradually subjectivising all internal experience —slowly enforcing the idea that truth lay *beneath* the threshold of consciousness and that the vital principle of the Real subsists in individual experience. Following an age of reason in which the principle of consciousness was a rational, calculating (and devisive) process of reflexive thought, this subsequent conception along organic lines did however allow imagination to regain a vital, creative, if *sub*-conscious, role once more.

This association of creativity with the unconscious permitted the Romantics to superimpose a passive 'feeling accord' upon the very nature that gave rise to it. It was significant that in referring to imagination as a 'co-adunating' faculty (a 'joining together'—from botany and physiology) Coleridge turned away from a symbolic cosmology and towards the model of physical science in order to formulate his analogy. This achieved a 'joining together' of the disparate elements from the flux of sense impressions to create forms whose substratum none the less, remains in the natural world. Sections III and IV of his Dejection Ode show the poet struggling with the matrix of Cartesian dualism with his recognition of its inadequacy. What would have enabled Coleridge to bridge this divide was a traditional analogical science of the soul providing not only a threefold cosmic structure of the material, subtle and intellectual worlds but also the spiritual means to grasp the symbolic forms of the mediatory realm where, as from the cosmic dream itself, archetypal rhythms prefigure all that takes form and shape in the natural world.

It is the soul's effective presence in this symbolic world that gives birth to analogical meaning in joining together the created world with the uncreated world of metaphysical essences, and not the reasoning *cogito* (whose presence is betrayed by the word *system* in the following passage) as Coleridge supposes in *The Statesman's Manual*:

In the Scriptures are the living educts of the imagination; of that reconciling and mediatory power, which, in incorporating the reason in images of sense, and organising (as it were) the flux of the senses by the permanence and self-circling energies of the reason, gives birth to a system of symbols, harmonious in themselves, and consubstantial with the truths of which they are the conductors.

It is instructive to compare this statement with a formulation of imaginative reality by the great Persian Master Suhrawardi.

[I]maginative forms exist neither in thought, since the great cannot be imprinted in the small, nor in concrete reality, otherwise anyone with normally healthy senses would be able to see them. But they are not merely non-being, for if so one could neither represent them to oneself, nor distinguish them one from another, and different judgements of them could not be formed. Since they are something with real being and are neither in thought, nor in concrete reality, nor in the world of the Intelligences—for they are corporealized forms, not pure intelligibles—they must necessarily exist in some other region and the latter is what is called the world of the *archetypal Image* and of *imaginative perception*. It is a world intermediate between the world of the Intelligence and the world of the senses; its ontological plane is above the world of the senses and below the intelligible world; it is more immaterial that the first, less immaterial than the second. It is a world in which there exists the totality of forms and figures, dimensions and bodies, with all that is connected therewith: movements, rest, positions, configurations, etc., all of them self-subsistent 'in suspense', that is to say, not being contained in a place nor depending on a substratum.[4]

In Coleridge's definition the transcendent source of symbolic, imaginative consciousness is shelved in favour of a 'mediatory power' organising sense impressions according to the method of reason. Doubtless, Coleridge, in common with the romantic movement in general, sought to re-establish the soul and its 'contents' as a valid spiritual principle but in this case his efforts were not sufficient to overcome the fact that no gnostic or metaphysical precedent was then effective in the West, which, had it existed, would have enabled him to reconcile two ideas which remained among his deepest concerns—his theory of imagination and the idea of man's moral freedom.

It is possible that without the work of Henry Corbin in bringing to our attention the gnostic, prophetic conception of the imagination at its highest and most subtle point of development, that the most profound possibilities of this *active* faculty would be lost to the West. Comparing Corbin's findings within the Iranian Illuminationist school from Avicenna to Mulla Sudra with Coleridge's thought enables us to see that, while for the latter imagination was a quasi-spiritual function, it was never for him entirely freed from a sensorial substratum. Imagination meant for Coleridge the natural world superimposed on an ideal world rather than, as it is in the traditional conception, this world seen in the light of its archetypal origins in the celestial realm.

In order to understand what is implied by this intermediate order of being we might turn to a passage from a Persian master of the nineteenth century.

It is a world which cannot be considered as being a part of our material universe, being clearly independent of the accidental matters of our universe and having a right of origin and a mode of subsistence peculiar to it, which do not derive from this material universe. The most that can be said is that with respect to it the matters of our world fulfill the function of a vehicle, of apparitional form, and of places in which to manifest. It has its own permanent existence above all these material realities. As in the case of the reflection manifested in a mirror: the image is other than the mirror, is distinct from the matter and form of the mirror. If the mirror is there, the image appears in it, if the mirror is not there, your silhouette and your image continue nonetheless to subsist through your person, without having anything to do with the mirror. It is exactly the same in the case of the world of the *barzakh*, the interworld. This world has its own independent existence; if the temporal and accidental matters of our world are there, the reflection of its image appears in them; if they are not there it continues to exist in its own 'place' and to subsist, thanks to the Soul. It simply means that it no longer has a form in which it can appear in the earthly material world. To recapitulate, there is the world of the *barzakh*, a world which exists and is permanent; it is invisibly, suprasensibly within our world, and it corresponds to it insofar as all the universes taken as a whole *symbolize with* one another.[5]

Again, in the light of such a passage it becomes evident that by comparison Coleridgean imagination is a re-presentation of the images of sense whereas the gnostic texts recovered by Corbin refer to a 'presentational knowledge'. That is to say, for Coleridge the world of imagination is dependent upon, and is fashioned after, the mode of psycho-sensual experience. But in the forms of the *active* imagination, the soul, as a spiritual presence, is situated on an inspirational plane that has no need of the imposition of forms from the material world. We may recall that in practice Coleridge found it necessary to posit, in contrast to 'fancy', a 'secondary Imagination' at work in the act of creation; one that does not, in Corbin's phrase, 'create being' (ascribe to its object full ontological certitude), so much as 'dissolves, diffuses, dissipates . . . in order to recreate' (Coleridge) from meditating on the impressions of nature.

Coleridge's attempt to recover the soul as a valid spiritual principle, in common with the aspirations of the 'romantic revolt' in general, really sprang from an awareness of the *feeling* accord between man and the 'beauteous forms of thing' (Wordsworth). But despite a recognition of the indwelling spirit of the beauties of virgin nature, far from yielding a science of symbols, natural forms are here idealised to form a series of mental sub-limations.

From the Renaissance to the end of the eighteenth century art looked increasingly to the 'classical' norms of abstraction and formal design based on observation, experiment and analysis of the natural world.[6] It was this trend that the romantic movement attempted to divert, not with any intention of deducing the inherent, logical forms of things, but to express the feelings, sentiments and associations that contemplation of nature could arouse. In neither case does the procedure go beyond the confines of sensory reaction in its means, and, in its effects, the stimulation of the individual's consciousness. But no artist can improvise from thought itself those cosmological operations that would effectively express the correspondence between the divine order and the human order of things and which forms the metaphysical precondition of spiritual imagination.[7] The aesthetic qualities of any work of art cannot claim a status of independence isolated from that metaphysical discernment between the Real and the illusory that is integral to all mental effort, for such a claim is without objective certitude in so far as it is confused with sense-perception and emotional reaction. This can be seen in the tendency of the Romantics to isolate nature from its interdependence with the total cosmic structure.[8]

The specific function of active imagination is to perceive as images the primordial and archetypal realities in which all common knowledge and experience ultimately subsists. In so doing all perception is linked through images, to the highest, innermost meaning and is the necessary pre-condition of spiritual regeneration. This is the significance of W.B. Yeats's interest in the occult (paralleling, at another level, the Romantic's interest in the natural world). His fondness for the byways of the psychic apart, Yeats hoped to discover in the Occult the hidden, imaginative laws of the world of *Anima Mundi*, or the 'Great Memory' as he sometimes called it. The symbols and images he found there he later in life related to metaphysical doctrines learned from his study of traditional doctrine, especially of the Vedanta, with the object of gaining a more conscious control and application of their powers. Moreover, Yeats is consistent with the traditional view in seeing the intermediate domain of subtle forms as containing the archetypal essences of the things of world. He was not subject to the error of supposing that the imagination has its features inferred or abstracted from the objects of sense. As he wrote in 1901 in his essay *Magic*: 'surely, at whatever risk, we must cry out that imagination is always seeking to remake the world according to the impulses and the patterns in that Great Mind and that Great Memory'.

In the late poetry of T. S. Eliot we can see the effect of the 'crisis' of imagination upon a deeply religious and poetic sensibility. His use of the *via negativa* in Four Quartets, gives expression to the implicit demands made upon a consciousness that operates in the absence of a vital, imaginative agent. Eliot possessed no spiritual 'vision' and attempted no poetic 'cosmology', as did, say, Blake. Nor was his sensibility rooted in an inherited racial tradition such as was Yeats's in Celtic folklore and legend. Eliot was in fact heir to the mainstream of European philosophic thinking, coming later to the orthodox doctrines of the Church, with a brief but important digression into Buddhist thought. Throughout the whole of his poetry there is a distinct note of irony in his expression of his own experience of the world. In such lines as these, from Burnt Norton,

> Desiccation of the world of sense,
> Evacuation of the world of fancy,
> Inoperancy of the world of spirit,

it is as if the imaginative faculty has been pulverised by an excessive rationality to allow a precise articulation of modern man's agnostic existentialism. The poet's choice of means to express adequately the lack of spiritual qualities in that experience is of interest in that the imaginative 'destitution' of the *via negativa* is more usually the vehicle of an ascetic spiritual path.

Compared with the imaginative restriction of Eliot's sensibility however, the expressive richness of the Romantic's attempt to find nature permeable to empathic observation takes on something of an embarrassing excess, and the visionary topography of a poet like Blake must seem like an eccentric fabrication. For an instructive contrast we might juxtapose the view of Shelley (for whom imagination was 'that imperial faculty'), who thought 'metrical language . . . a more direct representation of the actions and passions of our internal being', with Eliot's doubts as to the value of poetry as the vehicle of imaginative certainty, as expressed in these lines from East Coker:

That was a way of putting it—not very satisfactory:
A periphrastic study in a worn-out poetical fashion,
Leaving one still with the intolerable wrestle
With words and meanings. The poetry does not matter
It was not (to start again) what one had expected.
What was to be the value of the long looked forward to,
Long hoped for calm, the autumnal serenity
And the wisdom of age? Had they deceived us,
Or deceived themselves, the quiet-voiced elders,
Bequeathing us merely a receipt for deceit?
The serenity only a deliberate hebetude,
The wisdom only the knowledge of dead secrets
Useless in the darkness into which they peered
Or from which they turned their eyes.

We can sense a deep distrust as to the ontological certitude and objective value of imaginative perception in these lines. They are the expression of a creative sensibility that finds itself projected into a void between being and knowing. In this respect *Four Quartets* brilliantly articulates modern man's spiritual opacity, no less than the whole of Eliot's poetry reflects the quality of the modern intelligence that absents itself, as it were, from its own ultimate source.

A very different imaginative sensibility than that of Eliot's is revealed in the poetry of Vernon Watkins. Working with Watkins's drafts, Kathleen Raine has noted that they give evidence of his working for the 'elimination of naturalism on the one hand, and abstraction on the other'. But this need to work away from naturalism is yet a further indication of the problematic nature of imaginative perception for the modern mind. Although we have in the work of Vernon Watkins a poetry that expresses a metaphysics of vision (as we shall see in a later chapter) and an intimation of how the forms of nature may serve as symbolic types of their hidden essences; none the less, in steering a course between naturalism and abstraction there is the tacit avowal of the absence of a true science of symbols—of an analogical wisdom that in establishing the essential distinction between the Real and the illusory at the same time absolves the imagination of the error of imputing a 'false absoluteness' or an 'absolute transcience' to appearances.

It remains a question of some nicety to what extent the imaginative vision of the poets discussed in the following studies corresponds, in the final analysis, to the traditional analogical wisdom. What we are faced with is the challenge of understanding how the imaginative vision of these poets can form an effective beginning to an understanding of the soul's spiritual, imaginative function.

NOTES

1. See Henry Corbin, 'Mundus Imaginalis or the Imaginary and the Imaginal' in *Swedenborg and Esoteric Islam*, translated by Leonard Fox (Swedenborg Foundation, Pennsylvania, 1995), pp. 1–33.

2. In this realisation we are surely close to the wisdom that forms the first half of one of the aphorisms of Heraclitus: 'To God all things are beautiful, good, and right'. And in the notion that there is something intrinsically divisive, partial and exclusive in human knowledge when faced with the plenitude of the Divine Perfection, we have the completion of the aphorism: '. . . men, on the other hand, deem some things right and others wrong'. *Heraclitus*, by Philip Wheelwright (Oxford, 1959), p. 90.

3. In his exposition of the concept of Creative Imagination in relation to the theophanic doctrines of Ibn 'Arabi, Corbin notes that the primordial Being is a creative Being but insists that 'His creation springs, not from nothingness, from something other than Himself, from a not-Him, but from His fundamental being, from the potencies and virtualities latent in His own unrevealed Being'. Furthermore, 'here there is no notion of a *creatio ex nihilo* opening up a gulf which no rational thought will ever be able to bridge because it is this profoundly divisive idea itself which creates opposition and distance'. (*Creative Imagination*, op. cit., p. 185). However, as Frithjof Schuon points out, 'creative emanation . . . is not opposed to the theological idea of the *creatio ex nihilo*, but in fact explains its meaning'. *Dimensions of Islam*, translated by P. N. Townsend, (London, 1969), p. 153. And Titus Burkhardt supplies the explanation: 'The idea of creation, which is common to the three monotheistic religions, in appearance contradicts the idea of the essential Unity of all beings, since *creatio ex nihilo* seems to deny the pre-existence of possibilities in the Divine Essence and in consequence to deny also their subsistence in It, whereas the idea of manifestation as taught in Hinduism relates relative beings to Absolute Essence as reflections are related to their luminous source.

However, these two conceptions or symbolisms approach one another if we consider that the metaphysical meaning of the "nothingness" (*'udum*) whence the Creator "draws" things can only be the "nothingness" of "non-existence", i.e. of non-manifestation or the principial state, since the possibilities principially contained in the Divine Essence are not distinct in It as such before they are deployed in a relative mode. They are also not "existing" (mawjud) for existence already implies a first condition and virtual distinction of "knower" from "known".' See chapter 8 'Creation' in his *An Introduction to Sufi Doctrine*, translated by D. M. Matheson (Wellingborough, 1976).

4. See Corbin, *Spiritual Body and Celestial Earth: From Mazdean Iran to Shi'te Iran*, translated by Nancy Pearson (Princeton, 1977), p. 128.

5. This remarkable passage (taken from Corbin, *Spiritual Body*, p. 253) clearly indicates that the autonomous nature of the world of *barzakh* involves no dualism. Indeed, dualism only becomes a possibility when the continuity of the multiple degrees of being is, for whatever reason, destroyed.

6. By way of comparison we can point to a passage where Corbin cites an instance of a Persian master being able, in the presence of a devotee, to make the interior of a caravanserai of the beggars invisible in order to show him 'gardens, flower beds and streams of fresh water all around him'. See his *Spiritual Body*, op. cit., p. 264.

7. That Coleridge was aware of the need for such a pre-condition seems to be suggested in his hope that Wordsworth's projected philosophic poem would reveal it. See his *Letters*, Vol. 2., ed. E. J. Coleridge, (1895), p. 649. See also S. H. Nasr, *The Encounter of Man and Nature* (London, 1968), Chapter III, 'Some Metaphysical Principles Pertaining to Nature', and Frithjof Schuon, *The Transcendent Unity of Religions*, translated by Peter Townsend (London, 1953), Chapter IV, 'Concerning Forms in Art'.

8. 'It is too often overlooked that the word (Imagination) itself is the equivalent of Iconography. To imagine is to form an image of an idea, a thing in itself invisible; and this kind of "imitation" is the proper work of art . . . .. It presupposes not observation, but contemplation. The embodiment of concepts, fathered by Nous on Aisthesis, in the actual material of sound or pigment, calls for knowledge and precision, and that is where the Romantics so often fall short, by their exclusive reliance on feeling . . ..' A. K. Coomaraswamy, 'Letter to the Editor', *New English Weekly*, 14 June, 1945, p. 80.

II

Hamlet and Traditional Wisdom

thus we do of wisdom, and of reach,
With windlasses, and with assays of bias,
By directions find directions out.

Hamlet, 2.1.62–3[1]

BEYOND THE BRILLIANCE AND SEEMINGLY INEXHAUSTIBLE richness of the language, beyond any ambiguity of character and theme, what impresses us most about *Hamlet* is perhaps the multiplicity of its means. Like concentric, transparent spheres they interpenetrate and inform one another. Though never conflicting, each has its own elaboration of images which polarize around a single unifying centre. To penetrate to this centre requires not so much that we dig into the textual surface as bring to it a form of wisdom that will enable us to understand the play's total implications in the terms of a symbolism possessing an affiliation with a cosmological order of things. As Martin Lings, in his illuminating study of the later plays, has pointed out, 'Shakespeare's plays cannot be considered as sacred art in the full and central sense of the term, but they can be considered an extension of it, and as partaking both of its qualities and its functions.'[2]

The play embodies a meaning the communication of which requires the reader to see beyond characterisation. Only when the characters are seen as players of symbolic themes, does the play take on something of its full stature. We have in the character of Hamlet something more than just a railing and the beginnings of an individualist criticism as one commentator has suggested. A deeper and much more earnest issue is at stake. What Hamlet rails against is nothing less than a transformation that was taking place within the collective mentality of Shakespeare's time. It was the beginning of the development that, by

61

the eighteenth century, sought to circumscribe metaphysical intellect by human reason. This transformation of the spiritual dimension of human understanding had its beginnings in the humanist tendency to see the world as it is experienced by the individual. This individualism led to a naturalism in which everything that lies above nature became, for that very reason, beyond the reach of the individual as such.

Hamlet adequately reflects this transformation of consciousness. It is precisely 'naturalism' in this context that makes the 'uses of this world' seem to him 'weary, stale, flat, and unprofitable'. That is the real nature

> Of Hamlet's transformation—so call it,
> Sith nor th'exterior nor the inward man
> Resembles that it was.
>
> 2.2.5–7

His is a constant state of anxiety concerning 'reality', what 'seems' (1.2.76) and what is 'true'; a perpetual concern with 'that within which passes show' (1.2.85). In his concern for an inviolate truth there is an awareness that if the State of Denmark were left exclusively to its own devices there would no longer be any question of truth at all but only a notion of 'reality' limited to the unfixed and unstable conditions of private existence—intelligence reduced to its most transient dimension manifesting itself in a social order that does not embody the metaphysical order of a heavenly paradigm. That is the sense in which the drama of Hamlet may be considered symbolic since, in order to convey its profoundest meaning, it depends upon the qualitative view of reality inherent in the cosmic law of correspondence.

There are specific lines in the text that one may point to as hinting at such an interpretation, chief among which is Hamlet's, 'Prompted to my revenge by heaven and hell' (2.2.58), where we can sense immediately that the whole thrust of the drama is propelled by the need for revenge, in the light of a violation of the law by virtue of which each individual life is seen to be linked together with cosmic existence so as to contribute to the total harmony that is the universal order. Thus the context in which we have to understand Hamlet's course of action— provided imperatively by the infernal wanderings of his father's spirit (1.5.10–13)—is less a matter of personal debt and more an involvement with the cosmic process upon which human destiny depends. There is a further clue to this in Hamlet's lines:

> The time is out of joint, O cursèd spite,
> That ever I was born to set it right!
>
> 1.5.188–89

As much as anything else, the play is about that spiritual apathy with which we, perforce, surround ourselves; in the words of Polonius:

> 'Tis too much proved, that with devotion's visage
> And pious action we do sugar o'er
> The devil himself.
>
> 3.1.47–9

No complacent 'indifferent honest' approach to our spiritual con- dition will stand as adequate bulwark against the dark dissembling forces of evil and corruption:

> sit still my soul, foul deeds will rise,
> Though all the earth o'erwhelm them, to men's eyes.
>
> 1.2.258–59

Such lines as these go far beyond the human drama of the theatre to reach into the cosmic drama in which we all partake.

We have come to see that the medieval world-view holds a much greater place in the Renaissance period than was previously suspected, and although that earlier world-view had undergone some alteration of emphasis, all the late plays of Shakespeare have elements in common with its intrinsically metaphysical doctrines. In a general sense, both

Hamlet and his play span the medieval view and that of the Elizabethan age which adulterated medieval intellectuality with an 'individualism' that mingled knowledge of the divine with the beginnings of a profane understanding of the natural world. As Douglas Bush noted, 'By 1600, the time of Hamlet, the finest minds, grown restless and sceptical, are able to question traditional beliefs, to entertain the idea of life as meaningless flux, and to explore the depth of human corruption.' It was beginning to be more common for men to subject their own mental activity to rational analysis. The 'new science'—nothing less than the secularisation of thought that had the effect, eventually, of replacing a qualitative world-view with a quantitative one—certainly did 'call all in doubt'. The Cartesian dualism fell upon prepared ground.

Shakespeare was fully aware of the impulse that was a gradual surrender by the collective intelligence of his time to a view of reality as the 'knowing' process of individual and subjective reactions to the flow of events and appearances. This shift of cognitive emphasis lost the deeper penetration of the medieval view where, for instance, the Divine origin and source of the world seems itself guaranteed by the objects it manifests and where the external world, for all its substantiality, has none the less a certain transparency which situates the percipient within the fabric of a more total vision.[3]

The theatre that Shakespeare had as his heritage was still a comparatively recent innovation and differed radically from the traditions of the Mystery and Morality plays. It saw its main function as one of creating illusion, presenting, as Anne Righter has said, 'a self-conscious illustration of a thesis about reality'. Hamlet is a very 'theatrical' play in this sense, being much concerned with the nature of drama, 'whose end both at the first, and now, was and is, to hold as 'twere the mirror up to nature, to show virtue her own feature, scorn her own image, and the very age and body of the time his form and pressure'. (3.2.20–4) By now actors were famed for their ability and power to create the illusion of 'another' reality. But that other reality was a simulated version, albeit often in a different historical and social context, of the reality circumscribed by common sense. It involved, on the part of the audience, a certain duality of vision which allowed a brief respite or escape into a fictional world. This faculty of double vision, highly developed in Shakespeare's audiences, would have been all but unknown to the audience of the Mystery Play. The innovations of Elizabethan dramatic techniques by their very nature oppose their Medieval counterpart. Elizabethan 'characters' represent men and women playing at that general experience we call 'life', whereas in the Mystery Play the actors do not so much express 'life' as externalise or act out the dictates of the inner world of the Spirit—that is, they *objectivize* those hidden, intangible forms that impress the very pattern of that life. Elizabethan theatre, as nearly all theatre since, embodies a passive spectator consciousness and plays upon the emotions and feelings of the individual. But the Mystery Play moves us in order to convince us of the rightness of our involvement with what lies beyond and above our private existence—what gives it its being. All the complex ambiguity of the relationship between what 'seems' and what is true or 'real' in a play such as *Hamlet* would have been wasted on a Medieval audience.

Shakespeare's *Hamlet* is a microcosm, an extended and active poetic symbol in dramatic terms of the states of being that a man might know. The clue is supplied by Patrick Crutwell: 'one feels that the meaning which Shakespeare is striving to express is almost beyond the capacity of a drama filled only with human "characters".'[4] Such 'characters' in *Hamlet* serve to mirror the states of being within the play's central figure, each of those nearest to him precipitating the realisation or resolution of these states.

Viewed thus, we are given the link to the play's symbolic function. Hamlet approximates to the medieval view of man as the mediating point between angel and beast. Fundamental to the Christian tradition that helped form this view is the doctrine that man is created in the image of God. Yet he is necessarily part animal through his involvement in created nature. At the same time he reflects the spiritual world, so that inviolate truth is not entirely closed to him; he has within a divine seed, that metaphysical nucleus as it were by which he might reach beyond the confines of his limited self to be *re*-minded of his higher origin. By this 'seed', that 'light that lighteth every man who cometh into the world', he has the means of redemption from having 'fallen' into the domain of animal nature. If this lesser self were the final arbiter of all it could possibly mean to be man, then there would be no need of Hamlet's question:

> What is a man,
> If his chief good and market of his time
> Be but to sleep and feed? a beast, no more:
> Sure he that made us with such large discourse,
> Looking before and after, gave us not
> That capability and god-like reason
> To fust in us unused.
>
> 4.4.34-9

Here, intrinsic to his conception of a 'god-like reason',[5] Shakespeare broaches what, from the traditional standpoint, is the interrelated doctrine of the two 'selves'.[6] Distinguished as Immortal Spirit or Self ('my heart's core' 3.2.71) and psycho-physical, mortal soul ('machine' 2.2.124), the former is the immutable, transcendent principle of which the latter is a transient and contingent shadow: Hamlet's 'mortal coil' (3.1.67). To ascribe any degree of absoluteness to the mortal or empirical self is, from the metaphysical standpoint, the fallacy of identifying the self-subsistent essence of Being itself with the constant flux and transformation of subjective experience. To embrace Truth, Being and Oneness man must transcend his cognitive involvement with fleeting appearances. It is the indistinct essence of our individuality that is the unchanging and objective witness to the flow of appearances. This Self it is the abiding vocation of man to discover. That Hamlet is aware of the issues involved is made clear as early as Act 1.

> I know not 'seems'.
> 'Tis not alone my inky cloak, good mother,

Nor customary suits of solemn black,
Nor windy suspiration of forced breath,
No, nor the fruitful river in the eye.
Nor the dejected haviour of the visage,
Together with all forms, modes, shapes of grief,
That can denote me truly. These indeed seem,
For they are actions that a man might play,
But I have that within which passes show.

1.2.77–85

Whereas the means of discernment between the Real and the illusory are ultimately provided by the objective and transcendent Self, the psycho-physical self witnesses merely the 'show' of a level of reality that only 'seems', in being contingent upon the Absolutely Real (on pain of its projection into a nothingness). Moreover, this 'seeming' reality is apprehended by faculties which are themselves unreal in relation to the innermost essence of the knowing subject. Thus appearances, far from liberating the mind, imprison it and, losing their dimension of depth, become, in Hamlet's words, 'stale' and 'flat'. The world assumes the aspect of a 'sterile promontory' where the mind is subject to continual psychic disturbance. This is the web in which Hamlet finds himself enmeshed, for with the theme of individual redemption, Shakespeare has woven the analogous and necessary theme of the nature of 'reality' and 'illusion' as it affects the condition of man's ultimate destiny.

A necessary corollary of the fundamental doctrine of Self and ego is that the latter 'must put itself to death' (Blake's words). Only by an effective alignment of the soul to the integral demands of the Spirit can the inadequacies of our individuality be redeemed. This implies a recognition that the psycho-physical self must penetrate beyond what 'seems' if it is not to serve as the earthly veil that literally obscures the Real from the illusory. This is more easily appreciated, if, as Frithjof Schuon points out, one distinguishes in the Cosmos two poles, the one existential, blind and passive, and the other intellectual, therefore conscious and actual: matter is the point of precipitation in relation to the existential pole only, while the intellectual pole gives rise, at the extreme limit of the process of flight from God, to that 'personifiable force', or that perverted consciousness, who is Satan or Mara. In other words, Matter is the existence most remote from pure Intelligence, the divine Intellect . . . on the intellectual plane this remoteness can only spell subversion and opposition.[7]

Hamlet's isolation is created by his awareness that he alone properly understands what is involved in such a polarity. His speech to Guildenstern in Act 2, which includes the famous 'What a piece of work is man' (2.2.297–314), indicates, metaphorically, his involvement in 'sin'.

Hamlet himself is fallen Man—fallen from Adamic Being itself into conditioned, relative existence—the human existential state. The 'world' of the play—the state of Denmark—in effect contains every potentiality that belongs to the destiny of the human individual. The multiple states of being, as they are operative in human consciousness, must be brought into harmony by virtue of the law of correspondence, according to which every individual thing is linked to cosmic existence. The domain of virgin nature is potentially an earthly paradise, and is the symbolic manifestation of the uncreated, unmodified Adamic state. Moreover the law of correspondence points to the continuity of universal causality conjoining the multiple states of being. On the social plane the central principle of this continuity is the office of the King: 'Long live the king' refers to the office of Kingship and not to its temporary occupant. Owing to his unique position in the potential paradise of the natural world, the King is the earthly type of the Eternal Being: a terrestrial symbol of the absolute plenitude and goodness of God. He sustains the authority of the Spirit, but in terms of temporal power. When Hamlet says 'I am too much in the Sun' (1.2.67) he is alluding to this authority, but in its corrupt state. Through the power of kingship the possibilities inherent in what transcends man's natural state are extended and applied to the very form of the human collectivity, so that each individual within the order has every chance of having his particular destiny shaped and illuminated, either directly or indirectly, by the Supreme Power of Heaven. Shakespeare's description of this cosmic principle of kingship, utilising the symbol of the wheel, is put into the mouth of Rosencrantz in Act 3.

> The single and peculiar life is bound
> With all the strength and armour of the mind
> To keep itself from noyance, but much more
> That spirit upon whose weal depends and rests
> The lives of many. The cess of majesty
> Dies not alone; but like a gulf doth draw
> What's near it with it. O, 'tis a massy wheel
> Fixed on the summit of the highest mount,
> To whose huge spokes ten thousand lesser things
> Are mortised and adjoined, which when it falls,
> Each small annexment, petty consequence,
> Attends the boist'rous ruin. Never alone
> Did the king sigh, but with a general groan.
>
> 3.3.11–23

Now the cosmic order has been violated by the murder of Hamlet's father. His office has been taken from him by subversive means so that the existing order has broken down. Thus the forces of 'perverted consciousness' are given free play and threaten destruction, hence the many references to forms of contagion and disease hidden from view while on the surface everything *appears* to be in order. With the reign of disorder, 'the age is grown so picked, that the toe of the peasant comes so near the heel of the courtier' (5.1.135–37). Moreover

> . . . in the fatness of these pursy times
> Virtue itself of vice must pardon beg.
>
> 3.4.153–54

69

This is the inevitable consequence of what Hamlet announced at the end of Act 1, Scene 2;

> sit still my soul, foul deeds will rise,
> Though all the earth o'erwhelm them, to men's eyes
>
> 1.2.258–59

while its effect upon individual consciousness is described by the King in Act 4;

> the people muddied,
> Thick and unwholesome in their thoughts and whispers.
>
> 4.5.80–1

Through the free play of the forces of subversion and opposition in the 'state of Denmark', the earthly paradise has become 'an unweeded garden' (1.2.135) with its inhabitants guilty of the cardinal sin of indifference to the demands of an ultimate knowledge of the true order of things. They are, in Hamlet's terms, no more than merely 'indifferent honest'—that is to say morally passive and without active, spiritual vigilance. Having no longer access or effective contact with the spiritual order of reality, the garden,

> grows to seed, things rank and gross in nature
> Possess it merely.
>
> 1.2.136–37

Moreover, what should be an earthly paradise reflecting the Divine Will and Intelligence has become for Hamlet a state of impoverished consciousness; 'for there is nothing either good or bad, but thinking makes it so: to me it is a prison'. (2.2.252–54)

It is in moods that have become habitual and in acts that are motivated by nothing more than unthinking custom that man comes to sense the depreciation of his responses to the quality of things. This is the significance of Hamlet's 'damned custom' (3.4.36), which obscures the need to secure an attachment to one's ultimate spiritual destiny. The task from which Hamlet cannot rest is to see his acts reflect to the full extent he is capable of, the Divine purpose. That is why 'the king is not with the body. The king is a thing' (4.2.26–7). For the King is not King by virtue of his social position but only inasmuch as he reflects the authority of Heaven. The soul that has lost all sense of this paradigmatic correspondence lives in a perpetual 'bestial oblivion' (4.4.40) that is a parody of the true life.

The usurper then, 'a king of shreds and patches' (3.4.103), instead of reflecting spiritual authority, violates the conditions essential to sustain harmony and equilibrium in the terrestrial order. There is discord between Heaven and earth so that 'the time is out of joint' (1.5.188). The potential earthly paradise, 'this goodly frame' (2.2.302), grows 'rank' and 'unweeded'. 'That monster custom' (3.4.161) 'calls virtue hypocrite' (3.4.43). Man, from being 'noble in reason . . . infinite in faculties . . . like an angel in apprehension' becomes merely the 'paragon of animals' (2.2.308–11) and inhabits what for Hamlet is nothing 'but a foul and pestilent congregation of vapours' (2.2.306–7).

It is Hamlet's destiny to arrest this state of decay (but only by gradual steps that culminate in his death and not before certain 'rites of purification' have been effected), for he is involved in the cosmic hierarchy by virtue of his Princedom and his relationship to the Queen. Since the usurper's temporal power no longer reflects the infinite *mercy* of Heaven, the Devil feeds and multiplies within the contagious disorder. Those nearest Hamlet are like aspects of his own soul that devise means to procrastinate in various forms of distraction, fear, bodily comfort and the like. Meanwhile, Hamlet does nothing, appalled at how his course of revenge must involve his mother so that he is held back by a conscience that 'does make cowards of us all' (3.1.83). Recognising his own capacity for weakness, he confesses to Ophelia, 'I am myself indifferent honest, but yet I could accuse me of such thing, that it were better my mother had not borne me: I am very proud, revengeful, ambitious, with more offences at my beck, than I have thoughts to put them in' (3.1.123–27).

Among his distractions are his mother, who wants him to marry Ophelia, and Ophelia herself who wants some outward confirmation of what she hopes is Hamlet's love for her. Claudius wants Hamlet to remain

> Here in the cheer and comfort of our eye,
> Our chiefest courtier, cousin, and our son.
>
> 1.2.116–17

All these things urge him to a state of 'indifferent honest' ease away from his destiny. But in the name of what is ultimately Real Hamlet must revenge his father's death. Until equilibrium is restored there can be no rest, and through all vicissitudes he holds to his destiny. He realises that 'some must watch while some must sleep.' (3.2.273) Even as the angels watch over man's sleep, so must there always be someone to fight against the powers of darkness. Triumph over evil can never be taken for granted. Hamlet is always on guard, always restless and questioning, even while the forces of opposition, in the shape of Claudius, Rosecrantz and Guildenstern are ranging themselves against him.

> 'Tis now the very witching time of night,
> When churchyards yawn, and hell itself breathes out
> Contagion to this world.
>
> 3.2.391–93

His destiny involves, inextricably, not only the destiny of those who surround him, but more important, the destiny of those yet to come, a fact he cannot escape.

To the extent that a man is ignorant of his essential nature, he cannot actualise the Divine potential that is his by virtue of his creation in human form. Thus he slides helplessly towards the condition of sin, that unknowingness that lives on borrowed time and pays heavily at the Last Judgement. It is such a thought, coupled with the realisation that his destiny involves others, that urges Hamlet towards what, in all its enormity and horror, looks like too drastic a solution:

> But that the dread of something after death,
> The undiscovered country, from whose bourn
> No traveller returns, puzzles the will,
> And makes us rather bear those ills we have,
> Than fly to others that we know not of?
>
> 3.1.78–82

This is the substance of his time-honoured soliloquy. Do we resolve to identify our own existential being with the divine nature, in which case we must wage constant war upon all that deflects us from the difficult inner path, or do we remain content with the 'bestial oblivion' of the ego, passively suffering 'The slings and arrows of outrageous fortune'. (3.1.58) But the question arises: when we give up the ghost, in whom, when we go forth, shall we go forth? If there is no coincidence of mortal self with immortal Spirit, what does the 'sleep of death' hold for us 'When we have shuffled off this mortal coil' (3.1.67)—the void of nothingness or hell?

There is, then, only the one course of action—revenge! Heaven has been outraged by the murder and only by a complete exorcism can the cosmic harmony be restored. The operation must be irrevocable, with no compromise to the weakness of individual sentiment. Hamlet's failure to act entails his damnation:

> is't not to be damned,
> To let this canker of our nature come
> In further evil?
>
> 5.2.68–70

He must precipitate a revenge upon Claudius, who in the play personifies the 'perverted forces of consciousness', but which in reality are aspects of Hamlet's own soul. For like all spiritual dramas, Hamlet's inner drama must be played out upon the lonely stage of the soul.

His casting off of Ophelia comes at the crucial point in the drama at which he precipitates his future course of action. In addressing her thus:

> —Nymph, in thy orisons
> Be all my sins remembered
>
> 3.1.88–9

Hamlet recognises the terrible price his mortality exacts from him. His rejection of Ophelia is as much a revenge upon himself, for in mirroring his own soul Ophelia reminds him of his own involvement with the general contagion of the state of Denmark. An attachment to Ophelia would only weaken his resolve, which must remain inviolate. He is afraid that the power of her 'beauty will sooner transform' his honesty with himself 'from what it is to be a bawd' (3.1.111–12). The poignancy of his alternating 'I did love you once' and 'I loved you not' (3.1.115 and 119) is sharpened by the realisation that in renouncing Ophelia he is sacrificing the last possible source of solace within himself from 'the sea of troubles' that surrounds him.

Nor can there be any question of forgiving Claudius whose

> offence is rank, it smells to heaven
> It hath the primal eldest curse upon't,
> A brother's murder!
>
> 3.3.37–9

As for Hamlet's mother, his birthright duty demands of him that he pay respect to the fact that he is of her flesh and blood. Even so, he must turn her eyes into her 'very soul' so that she may see that she too has been infected with

> such black and grainéd spots
> As will not leave their tinct.
>
> 3.4.90–1

Even his procrastination serves the purpose of discovering the extent to which the King's immediate 'constellation' of subjects has defiled the 'garden' and

> spread the compost on the weeds
> To make them ranker.
>
> 3.4.151–52

Claudius, who personifies the forces of opposition and subversion in Hamlet's own nature, must undergo a period of infernal wandering, prefiguring his final descent to Hell, so that the extent of his guilt is fully fathomed.

Despite Hamlet's procrastination, everything about this drama points to his death as being the consummation of an inexorable destiny. When the play closes at his Judgement he has engineered his own redemption in a Self-knowledge which will prove the foundation-stone of his certainty at having restored cosmic harmony to the state of Denmark, and having gained rightful command over the forces of perverted consciousness. He has triumphed over illusion, having won through to a level of being commensurate with his 'god-like reason'. He has attained the discernment of his naked soul:

> Since my dear soul was mistress of her choice,
> And could of men distinguish.
>
> 3.2.61–2

In the light of his newly attained knowledge, *created* nature becomes transparent to *creative* Being. (This accounts for his concern with the processes of nature, whereby 'a king may go a progress through the guts of a beggar' (4.3.29–30), such 'progress' representing for the Prince merely the transient modification of ultimate reality.) The revenge completed, and with the arrival of Fortinbras, cosmic harmony is restored. The task finished—'Now cracks a noble heart. Good night, sweet prince' (5.2.357)—his lonely destiny is truly fulfilled.

But what of Hamlet's death in relation to the doctrine of the two 'selves' with its metaphysical corollary, the objective discernment of the abiding nature of the Real? From early on in the play, though at first for no explicit reason, we sense that Hamlet's death will be necessary in the sequence of events that are to follow. To appreciate this fully we need to understand just how these doctrines, when interrelated, interpret the nature of death. There is a profound reason why Hamlet struggles to grasp the dualistic nature of the Real and the illusory as it affects his own conscious destiny. From the viewpoint of what Schuon has called the existential pole, at death the generated body does not cease to be existential but is so transformed that 'A man may fish with the worm that hath eat of a king, and eat of the fish that hath fed of that worm' (4.3.26–7). Thus life is woven out of death and death from life. Hamlet reflects on this process at Ophelia's grave—'Alexander died, Alexander was buried, Alexander returneth to dust, the dust is earth, of earth we make loam' (5.1.204–5).

From the viewpoint of what Schuon calls the intellectual pole, however, if at the point of death the individual being is not to be claimed by the powers of darkness, the immutable essence must be identified with its connatural agent, the Divine Intelligence it serves to reflect. For only in accordance with their integral and consubstantial nature can the condition of individuality be reconciled to the inviolate truth that is ultimate unity. Not only must Hamlet die clear of the guilt at having done nothing to revenge the devil in the shape of Claudius, but he must also be free from the accrued limitations of his lower self. His higher Self must be at peace by being properly situated in the cosmic harmony, so that when at death he 'goes forth' his passage is unhindered by unresolved residues of his 'mortal coil'.

Stripped of what 'seems' the ultimate earthly possession—his individual personality—and provided we make the symbolic transposition proposed at the outset of this study—the 'poverty' of Hamlet's death can be seen in Christian terms as one of spiritual preparation and purity. Having been urged by every mode and manner of a corrupt Court (that itself prefigures the cosmic separation of man's conditioned existence on earth) to renounce all spiritual valour in favour of the rewards that accrue to earthly comfort, his is no less the archetypal Christian choice of spiritual redemption by way of an earthly renunciation: 'There is no man that hath left house, or brethren, or sisters, or father, or mother, or wife, or children, or lands, for my sake, and the gospel's, but he shall receive an hundredfold now in this time, houses and brethren, and sisters, and mothers, and children, and lands, with persecutions; and in the world to come eternal life' (Mark 10.29–30).

Shakespeare indicates the transition from earthly existence to heavenly life in Hamlet's concern for his reputation in this world; for such a reputation can only have meaning and veracity by the terms of a purification of the soul before its entry into a world that not only in every respect entirely transcends this one, but is indeed its very source. As evidence that the transition is effected we are given the line 'And flights of angels sing thee to thy rest' (5.2.359), which we can suppose implies that the disequilibriums that constitute the fabric of the drama are synthesised into a state of complete equilibrium that itself is a symbol of the total cosmic harmony as it mirrors the state of Heaven Itself.

NOTES

1. References throughout are to the New Cambridge Shakespeare, *Hamlet*, edited by John Dover Wilson (Cambridge, 1968).

2. *Shakespeare in the Light of Sacred Art* (London, 1966) p.27.

3. In this respect the reader might compare a Shakespeare sonnet with the fourteenth century lyric with the refrain, 'This world fareth as a fantasy', see *Medieval English Lyrics*, ed, by R. T. Davies (London, 1963) p.127. With Shakespeare's sonnets the *passive* feelings and responses of the individual are allowed a determining role and given a quasi-absoluteness unthinkable in the earlier epoch.

4. *The Shakespearean Moment* (London, 1954) p.102.

5. We recall that the word 'reason', like its companion 'speech', has its semantic links with the Greek *Logos*.

6. 'I was in two minds', 'I was beside myself' and 'self control' are current expressions that mirror, albeit in some shadowy way, this timeless doctrine.

7. See Frithjof Schuon, *In The Tracks of Buddhism*, trans. by Marco Pallis (London, 1968) p.57.

III

Myself Must I Remake

Grant me an old man's frenzy.
Myself must I remake
Till I am Timon and Lear
Or that William Blake
Who beat upon the wall
Till Truth obeyed his call.

'An Acre of Grass'

I

READING OVER THE BODY OF HIS WRITINGS, WE MUST CON-
clude that as a young man Yeats had some momentary intuition of the
supreme mystery and then spent the rest of his life tirelessly tracing out
every implication of that moment. This process came to represent for
him a constant striving to embody in the fullest possible sense what he
called Unity of Being. Every subsequent effort to attain self-realisation
was spurred on by the rule, 'Hammer your thoughts into a Unity'.

Yeats belonged to that small body of thinkers of the nineteenth
century—themselves heir to that 'alternative', hermetic philosophy
begun at the Renaissance—who had come to believe that the so-called
Enlightenment of Europe was a form of idolatry based upon the false
premise of mind in opposition to matter. 'Three provincial centuries'
(as the philosopher A. N. Whitehead called them) had made impossible
—on the premises they allowed to prevail—a unifying perspective such
as Yeats sought. In a letter written in May 1926 to his friend Sturge
Moore, Yeats gave his retrospective view of those centuries:

In the seventeenth century people said [that] our senses are responsible for colour, scent and sound, and that colour, scent and sound
are 'appearances' but that mass and movement really exist. In the
eighteenth century one or two men pointed out that mass and
movement are just as much 'appearances,' because the invention of
our senses, as colour, scent and sound. Then a little later it was discovered that the organs themselves—the organs as observed as
objects of science—are part of the 'appearances': we see the eye
through the eye. From that moment we were back in ancient philosophy and must deduce all from the premises known to Plato.

Yeats's 'revolt of the soul against intellect' sought to embody Unity
through that symbolic knowledge in which truth inheres on the side
of essence instead of on the side of fact, and his gradual mastery of the
symbolic wisdom of imaginative knowledge transformed him into one
of the great, learned poets of European literature.

For Yeats, Blake was 'the first writer of modern times to preach the
indissoluble marriage of all great art with symbol' and who, in so
doing, 'announced the religion of art', the only possible religion that in
the modern world could 'make our souls' after the heart's acknowledgement of the divine impulse of beautiful things. Yeats aspired to
use that 'religion' as a path to his own perfection. In 1898 at the age of
33 he wrote in his essay 'The Autumn of the Body':

The arts are, I believe, about to take upon their shoulders the bur-
dens that have fallen from the shoulders of priests, and to lead us
back upon our journey by filling our thoughts with the essences of
things, and not with things. We are about to substitute once more
the distillation of alchemy for the analyses of chemistry and for
some other sciences; and certain of us are looking everywhere for the
perfect alembic that no silver or golden drop may escape.

The 'religion of art' was to take upon itself the task of renewing
man's contact with the immutable realities. Then, like the alchemist, it

could speak of the redemption of souls and reject science's cumulative knowledge of the external.

The problem of the relation of knowledge to consciousness had a recurring fascination for Yeats and he seems never to have credited the outer world with a greater degree of reality than the inner world. In his essay 'Magic' of 1901 he had written of his belief that 'the borders of the mind are ever shifting, and that many minds can flow into one another, as it were, and create or reveal a single mind, a single energy.' Some 25 years later, in March 1926, writing to Sturge Moore with whom at this time he was conducting a protracted correspondence on the relationship of consciousness to objective reality, he wrote:

> we have no longer the right to say that there is any image of the mind peculiar to one person: something of it is peculiar, a something of the images we call physical is peculiar, and that is all we can say. It becomes necessary to consider that all minds may make under certain circumstances a single mind.

By temperament he was ideally suited to the view—that of the wisdom he acquired by intense study of esoteric and hermetic doctrines—that reality and the very 'ground' of consciousness are consubstantial. In his essay 'The Symbolism of Poetry' of 1900 he wrote:

> I doubt indeed if the cruder circumstances of the world, which seems to create all our emotions, does more than reflect, as in multiplying mirrors, the emotions that have come to solitary men in moments of poetical contemplation; or that love itself would be more than an animal hunger but for the poet and his shadow the priest, for unless we believe that outer things are the reality, we must believe that the gross is the shadow of the subtle, that things are wise before they become foolish, and secret before they cry out in the market-place. Solitary men in moments of contemplation receive, as I think, the creative impulse from the lowest of the Nine Hierarchies, and so make and unmake mankind, and even the world itself, for does not 'the eye altering alter all'?

83

At odds as he was with most 'official' contemporary philosophical thinking, he came to hate with an ever greater degree of understanding a mentality that, in its passive submission to the senses, 'knows nothing because it has made nothing'. With Blake he repudiated Locke's 'Nothing in mind that has not come from sense' and welcomed Leibniz's retort 'nothing except mind'. With his passionate delight in the sensual flux of life he believed, as he wrote in 'Discoveries', the poet must

> find his pleasure in all that is forever passing away that it may come again, in the beauty of woman, in the fragile flowers of spring, in momentary heroic passion, in whatever is most fleeting, most impassioned, as it were, for its own perfection, most eager to return in its glory . . . [for] . . . the end of art is the ecstasy awakened by the presence before an ever-changing mind of what is permanent in the world, or by the arousing of that mind itself into the very delicate and fastidious mood habitual with it when it is seeking those permanent and recurring things.

Whenever such a viewpoint becomes impossible, then poetry itself must relinquish, as he put it in 'The Autumn of the Body', the 'right to consider all things in the world as a dictionary of types and symbols and [begin] to call itself a critic of life and an interpreter of things as they are'.

Yeats was very much a man of his time, both in the scepticism he inherited from his father and in his insistence on having practical confirmation at every stage of his experience. But he differed profoundly from his age in not attaching too much value of that *public* proof so often the absolute criteria of materialist assumptions. In his essay 'Bishop Berkeley' of 1931 he confessed:

> If you ask me why I do not accept a doctrine so respectable and convenient, its cruder forms so obviously resurrected to get science down from Berkeley's roasting-spit, I can but answer like

Zarathustra, 'Am I a barrel of memories that I should give you my reasons?' Somewhere among those memories something compels me to reject whatever—to borrow a metaphor of Coleridge's—drives mind into the quicksilver.

The poet's impatience with the methods of science arose from what he felt to be its inability to account for much of his own rich, inner experience. Having familiarised himself with magic, mediums, theosophy and other aspects of the occult he came in his thirty-second year to collect folklore. Discovering retrospectively the logic of his method he wrote in 'Swedenborg, Mediums and the Desolate Places': 'I was comparing one form of belief with another, and, like Paracelsus who claimed to have collected his knowledge from midwife and hangman, I was discovering a philosophy.' These interests converged at a time when he believed a significant part of the general mental outlook was turning away from a mechanised view of the world, and, no longer caught up with 'objects' was, as he wrote in 'The Autumn of the Body',

> beginning to be interested in many things which positive science, the interpreter of exterior law, has always denied: communion of mind with mind in thought and without words, foreknowledge in dreams and in visions, and in the coming among us of the dead, and of much else.

For Yeats at least, the worlds on both sides of the grave seemed to directly complement one another. His interest in occult phenomena arose from a desire to discover a hierarchy of intermediate spirits between man and the ultimate levels of the real; a need to confirm the inner laws of imaginative thought.

Later in life, especially in the years after he had prepared a revised edition of A Vision and was seeking a philosophical confirmation of its system, Yeats undertook a study of Greek philosophy. He wrestled long and hard with the problems of ontology, comparing his own beliefs with those of Plato and Plotinus and certain pre-Socratics as well as with later philosophers like Nicholas of Cusa, Berkeley, Whitehead, McTaggart and Gentile. Each stage of assimilation along his self-imposed 'path of perfection' was a step nearer realisation of Unity of Being.

Looking back over this struggle to construct a philosophy that would allow him direct access to the abiding source of all knowledge, it becomes apparent that a shift of emphasis was taking place. His earlier occult studies had a predominantly practical purpose. As he confessed in the Preface to the first edition of *A Vision*, he was laying down 'a system of thought that would leave my imagination free to create as it chose and yet make all it created, or could create, part of the one history, and that the soul's.' The effect of the deeper and more philosophic learning of his maturity gave his later thought an increasingly metaphysical cast. The poet felt the need for a cosmology at once traditional, universal, and confirming of his own experience of the life of the soul.

Having reached, by 1930, the penultimate stage of his search for Unity of Being in Neoplatonic metaphysics, in the final decade of his life the elderly poet came to embrace as the supreme doctrine of Unity, the Indian Vedanta. This he did with an enthusiasm that perhaps only an old man who has nothing to lose and everything to gain could feel (twice, in 1927 and in 1928, he had come close to death). This study set the crown upon his toiling for perfection and contributed the final link in his understanding. Here were those 'manuals of devotion' for which he had long sought and which now enabled him to bind together all he had experienced of the soul's destiny with doctrines concerning the very sources of the conscious mind. His discovery of a mythology in Faery Faith and Celtic Legend, the speculative symbols he borrowed from the rituals of the Golden Dawn and the Kabbalah, his study of Alchemy and Magic, the cosmology he won from years of close acquaintance with Swedenbourg and Boehme and various Greek philosophers—for all their subtlety and wealth of symbolic resonance, these were still inadequate to perfect concentration upon that Unity which was his ultimate goal.

In this final assault upon the Vedantic wisdom had he come to realise, with the *Bhagavad Gita*, that 'men of darkness are they, who make a cult of the departed and of spirits'? Certainly, he had singled out and was fond of quoting a passage from the Chaldean Oracles that seemed nothing if not a reproach for the years he had, periodically, spent 'upon Hodos Chameliontos': 'stoop not down to the darkly splendid world wherein lieth continually a faithless depth and Hades wrapped in cloud, delighting in unintelligible images.'[1]

In recognising the importance of this last stage of Yeats's search for Unity of Being, we have to acknowledge it as the culmination of an interest in Hindu doctrines from at least his twentieth year, when he met Mohini Chatterjee as a member of the Dublin Hermetic Society. He it was, as Yeats reports in 'Reveries over Childhood and Youth', who

> confirmed my vague speculations and seemed at once logical and boundless. Consciousness, he taught, does not merely spread out its surface but has, in vision and in contemplation, another motion and can change in height and in depth.

The impetus to undertake this final step was clearly provided by the poet's friendship with Shri Purohit Swami (they met in 1931) who could, from personal experience, tell the poet what meditations 'enrich the waking mind'. In outgrowing magic, seances, theosophy and science in wisdom, Yeats felt the need, more than ever before, for a 'coherent grasp of reality' which would unite all possible antinomies, from the great antinomy of the One and the Many down to the least that are the expression of delicate emotional states. And further, that these opposites be resolved in a unity of consciousness that, according to the terms of the system of *A Vision*, is the circle become sphere that 'can be symbolised but cannot be known'.

The poet was of course fully aware of the ancient lineage and universality of Vedanta, and he interpreted it as confirming his long held belief that it is the soul that makes and unmakes reality. Just as he had earlier hoped to establish a ritual order that would set before Irishmen a literature which could 'turn our places of beauty or legendary association into holy symbols', so, now, he was confident that his Irish ancestry gave him an honourable place within the perennial wisdom. He wrote, in 'A General Introduction for my Work', in 1937,

> I was born into this faith, have lived in it, and shall die in it; my Christ, a legitimate deduction from the creed of St Patrick as I think, is that Unity of Being Dante compared to a perfectly proportioned human body, Blake's 'Imagination,' what the Upanishads have named 'Self': nor is this unity distant and therefore intellectually understandable, but imminent, differing from man to man and age to age.

Such doctrines, he now believed, must be studied if the West was to escape the 'dangerous fanaticism' of those 'provincial centuries' that drove 'mind into the quicksilver'. From his Preface to The Ten Principal Upanishads (which he put into English with the Swami) we can see how Yeats hammered together his belief in the metaphysical universality of his own deepest intuitions in the light of the teachings of the Vedas:

> It pleases me to fancy that when we turn towards the East, in or out of Church, we are turning not less to the ancient west and north; the one fragment of pagan Irish philosophy come down, 'the Song of Amergin', seems Asiatic; that a system of thought like that of these books, though less perfectly organised, once overspread the world, as ours today; that our genuflections discover in that East something ancestral in ourselves, something we must bring into the light before we can appease a religious instinct that for the first time in our civilisation demands the satisfaction of the whole man.

An event in late 1931 gave a further intimation from personal experience of the nature of Unity of Being. In a letter to his old friend Olivia Shakespeare, he was ecstatic:

I went for a walk after dark and there among some great trees became absorbed in the most lofty philosophical conception I have found while writing *A Vision*. I suddenly seemed to understand at last and then I smelt roses. I now realised the nature of the timeless spirit. Then I began to walk and with my excitement came—how shall I say?—that old glow so beautiful with its autumnal tint. The longing to touch it was almost unendurable. The next night I was walking in the same path and now the two excitements came together. The autumnal image, remote, incredibly spiritual, erect, delicate featured, and mixed with it the violent physical image, the black mass of Eden. Yesterday I put my thoughts into a poem . . . but it seems to me a poor shadow of the intensity of the experience.

The poem was 'Crazy Jane and Jack the Journeyman'.

The exact nature of this realisation of a 'moment out of time', for obvious reasons, cannot be subjected to any scrutiny. But beyond doubt, that moment acted as a lodestone to the poet during the last decade of his life. He had, of course, long held that pure aesthetic experience was itself an intimation of such a moment free of time and fate. Some three years earlier, in a note intended for the revised *A Vision*, Yeats had described the 'moment' in terms of that book's system:

the point in the Zodiac where the whirl becomes a sphere once reached, we may escape from the constraint of our nature and from that of external things, entering upon a state where all fuel has become flame, where there is nothing but the state itself, nothing to constrain it or end it. We attain it always in the creation or enjoyment of a work of art, but that moment though eternal in the Daimon passes from us because it is not an attainment of our whole being.

For the poet upon the path of 'self-renewal' and perfection, the moment among the great trees came as a validation of an arduous struggle. Was this the culminating point towards which he had been drawn all his creative life? And, having reached it, did silence beckon? Was he to be 'a singer born and lack a theme . . . struck dumb in the simplicity of fire' as he wrote in 'Vacillation VII'? Certain things he wrote after the event suggest indeed that silence did beckon.

II

There was always something implicitly 'mystical' in Yeats's approach to life. In particular he seems increasingly to have looked on the 'outside' world—with perfect consistency to his metaphysics—with an eye to finding out what it could tell him of his own nature. This manifests itself in his desire to become, as it were, absolutely his 'Self' rather than merely himself.

The inner tensions of this aspiration heighten the imaginative energy of much of Yeats's later poetry and is present there by virtue of his desire to achieve 'radical innocence' while possessing the greatest possible knowledge of the world of sensual flux. By these diverse means the poet hoped to gain access to the centre of reality, a reality never merely subjective any more than crudely phenomenal. In 1938 he wrote to Ethel Mannin: 'All men with subjective natures move towards a possible ecstasy, all with objective natures towards a possible wisdom.' There can be no doubt that, for Yeats, Unity of Being meant reconciling these opposites. In 'Pages from a Diary in 1930', he wrote,

> I am always, in all I do, driven to a moment which is the realisation of myself as unique and free, or to a moment which is the surrender to God of all that I am . . .. Could those two impulses, one as much a part of truth as the other, be reconciled, or if one or the other could prevail, all life would cease . . .. The ultimate reality must be all movement, all thought, all perception extinguished, two freedoms unthinkably, unimaginably absorbed in one another.

For the student of his poetry, Yeats's approach to reality has many implications, not the least of which is that when the poetry seems to be at its most idiosyncratic it is often enunciating metaphysical doctrine with a symbolism that is at once specific, personal and universal. The imaginative world disclosed therein quite obviously has to be recognised according to its qualitative content. Not that this should lead us to suppose there is an explicable 'philosophy' waiting to be uncovered beneath the body of his poems; not even that of *A Vision*.

For Yeats both the creative act and its fruits—'monuments of unageing intellect'—foreshadow Unity of Being. In a passage in 'Discoveries' we can see how he envisaged the relationship of the creative act to the contemplation of the ultimate Unity by modifying the Augustinian symbol of God as the circle whose centre is everywhere but whose circumference is nowhere:

> If it be true that God is a circle whose centre is everywhere, the saint goes to the centre, the poet and artist to the ring where everything comes round again. The poet must not seek for what is still and fixed, for that has no life for him; and if he did, his style would become cold and monotonous, and his sense of beauty faint and sickly.

The saint may disdain the 'ordinary' experience of life and fall silent in contemplation of the mystery of his own being at the highest level of experience where, as he puts it in 'A Dialogue of Self and Soul',

> intellect no longer knows
> *Is* from the *Ought*, or *Knower* from the *Known*—
> That is to say, ascends to Heaven;
> Only the dead can be forgiven;
> But when I think of that my tongue's a stone.

But if the saint's path to the ultimate reality of God is by way of renunciation of all that 'comes round again', the poet's path (spoken of in the penultimate stanza of the poem) is by way of discovering the sanctity of the artist's creative power to reveal the abiding relation between what passes and the dimensionless point or divine centre upon which it depends and around which it revolves:

> I am content to follow to its source
> Every event in action or in thought;
> Measure the lot; forgive myself the lot!
> When such as I cast out remorse
> So great a sweetness flows into the breast
> We must laugh and we must sing,
> We are blest by everything,
> Everything we look upon is blest.

Tracing the pattern of Yeats's own spiritual development as reflected in the increasing self-possession and power of his imaginative thought, we find in the early poems such as 'The Indian Upon God' that God is affirmed mirror-fashion, taking the hue and cast of each and every reflection of itself in multiplicity. Yet later in 'Mohini Chatterjee' we find God affirmed as that 'nothing' which is the Unity that 'contains' yet is not involved in the movement of all transient things. Later still, embodied in the Supernatural Song 'A Needle's Eye', we discover a characteristic of the later Yeats where God, as the eternal and fecund source of everything that has life, seems also the very source and being of the creative act itself:

> All the stream that's roaring by
> Came out of a needle's eye;
> Things unborn, things that are gone,
> From needle's eye still goad it on.

The needle's eye holds not only the thread of destiny (woven by shrouds in 'Cuchulain Comforted') but is also the golden thread of the supernal sun (immutable spirit) that fatefully stitches together all things.

The needle's eye is also, by symbolic transposition, the all-seeing eye of the Divine Intellect ('the lonely height where all are in God's eye', of 'Paudeen'), again the centre point of the circle whose circumference is everywhere. From this unmanifest point His creations are descried as a circuit that revolves around Him and within Him. It is thus, in its inclusive richness, a symbol of the coincidence of contraries of scale that is one of the symbols of God's Infinity.

The same symbol appears in 'Veronica's Napkin', a poem that signals a shift of emphasis in the poet's religious imagery from pagan transcendence to Christian immanence.

> The Heavenly Circuit; Bernice's Hair;
> Tent-pole of Eden; the tent's drapery;
> Symbolic glory of the earth and air!
> The Father and His angelic hierarchy
> That made the magnitude and glory there
> Stood in the circuit of a needle's eye.

In this opening section of the poem all created things of 'earth and air' are symbolic types of the 'Heavenly Circuit' supported by the *axis mundi*. They embody the divine prototype in the 'magnitude and glory' of symbolic consonance, and all within the still and 'distant' scrutiny of God's transcendent gaze. Yeats began an earlier poem, 'He Wishes for the Clothes of Heaven', with the line 'Had I the heaven's embroidered cloths', but the imagery does not betray the depth of symbolic resonance his later mastery could summon.[2]

The transcendent cosmology of these lines is placed in contrast to the immanence of the last two by a simple reference to the napkin used to wipe Christ's face on the path to Calvary. The symbol makes it immediately apparent that the miracle of God is tangibly present in the imprint upon the napkin.

> Some found a different pole, and where it stood
> A pattern on a napkin dipped in blood.

This immanence of the Divine Principle seen as being plunged directly into the particular and personal life is reflected in the group of Crazy Jane poems written soon after 'Veronica's Napkin' in 1929. Their themes are at once timeless and immediate, now cosmic in implication, now full of the passion of human life. Yet, as the refrain from 'Crazy Jane on God' has it, *All things remain in God*.

As well as reflecting something of his acquired Neoplatonic doctrine of the soul, the Crazy Jane poems express a desire for something dynamic the poet had felt a few years earlier: 'a movement downwards upon life not upwards'. They were written at an important juncture in his life and at a time when 'life returned to me as an impression of the uncontrollable energy and daring of the great creators', as he confessed in The Winding Stair and Other Poems. He now wanted belief from direct, personal experience, not assent to some philosophy: 'music not logic'.

In 'Crazy Jane talks with the Bishop', for instance, the poem's ostensible theme, the earthly rewards of human passion versus the altruistic rewards of religious morality in old age, is lifted to a new dimension by its last stanza when Crazy Jane, 'learned in bodily lowliness', is able to counter the Bishop's call to moral reform by suggesting that the 'foul sty' he would have her deny is from another viewpoint the 'heavenly mansion' of love itself. The Bishop's dogmatic locus for the place of redemption seems impoverished against that of Crazy Jane who has realised that the point of redemption is every 'where' where opposites are united and not, as the Bishop supposes, within the exclusive category of virtuous acts.

> A woman can be proud and stiff
> When on love intent;
> But Love has pitched his mansion in
> The place of excrement;
> For nothing can be sole or whole
> That has not been rent.

The whole poem might be seen as an extension of the theme of

'Consolation', written some two years earlier, where in the second of the two stanzas the soul's virginal innocence prior to its decent—and therefore loss—into generation is recaptured at the moment out of time at the height of sexual union.

> How could passion run so deep
> Had I never thought
> That the crime of being born
> Blackens all our lot?
> But where the crime's committed
> The crime can be forgot.

Yeats's late mastery here is notable for the way in which the symbol of the coincidence of contraries that energises the whole poem permeates its imaginative texture like a veiled subtext. The identity of contraries (one of the most powerful and recurrent of Yeats's symbols) is deployed here to suggest that only in uniting what is opposite and asunder can the inclusiveness that is the very nature of Unity of Being escape the danger of any possible exclusion.[3]

The final phase of Yeats's approach to Unity of Being can be said to begin with his friendship with Shri Purohit Swami. This was the most important influence upon the poet in his remaining years. He had finished re-writing *A Vision* and, having read western philosophy for some years, was turning away from its over-rationalised, abstract vision of things and was searching for a more immediate grasp of reality: intuitive and physical at once. This was in fact his 'A Prayer for Old Age':

> God guard me from those thoughts men think
> In the mind alone;
> He that sings a lasting song
> Thinks in a marrow-bone.

As late as September of 1933 the poet could write to his friend Sturge

Moore that he was 'trying for new foundations'. His association with the Swami was timely in the laying of them.

The poems that most clearly reflect the new perspective, while embodying his continuing ambivalence towards Christian doctrine, is the group of Supernatural Songs. These poems are exceedingly rich because of Yeats's mastery at recapitulating, by implication, the vast store of his poetic thought. Here converge many of his recurrent themes; the male/female Divinity, the sexual act as opening upon the beatific vision, the internal Deity, the soul's successive rebirths, as well as his myth of 'radical innocence'. As a group the poems are a further exploration of the poet/saint antinomy; in them Yeats came nearest to resolving the antinomy in terms of the saint at the centre where all is fixed and still. They are the result of his turning for the third time in his life towards eastern doctrine.

Yeats's belief that the creative will of his art came from his combat with himself found its reflection in those eastern doctrines of self-realisation that, as we have seen, recovered something 'ancestral' in Man himself. This allowed him to associate in his own mind India with early Christian Ireland, a tradition of universal wisdom to which he belonged and which alone could, as the development in later centuries of institutional religion could not,[4] permit that unity of belief which had 'become so important to [his] inventions.'

In his Preface to *A Full Moon in March* Yeats described the central character of the Supernatural Songs, the hermit Ribh, as an orthodox man but for his ideas about the Trinity, an imaginary critic of St. Patrick whose Christianity, 'come perhaps from Egypt like much earlier Irish Christianity, echoes pre-Christian thought'. Ribh is, of course, also a mask that allows Yeats to unite in his imagination early Irish Christianity and Indian mysticism in a tradition of seeking the internal Deity.

The earlier title for 'Ribh denounces Patrick', 'Ribh prefers an older Theology', offers a clue to the poet's intention. Here Yeats is explicit in his preference for the earlier Christian doctrine of the internal, imma-nent God as against the abstraction of an external Deity. This later conception is for Yeats divisive, separating the divine and human worlds and resulting in a deprivation of the inclusive nature of the human state. The substitution of the exclusively masculine Trinity of Father, Son and Holy Ghost by the Divinity having both male and female powers, permits the symbolic correspondence between cosmogonic generation and transfigured sexual passion.

> Natural and supernatural with the selfsame ring are wed.
> As man, as beast, as an ephemeral fly begets, Godhead begets
>   Godhead,
> For things below are copies, the Great Smaragdine Tablet said.

The poet would have met with the doctrine of a male/female God not only in Indian thought but in his Kabbalistic and Platonic studies as well. In the person of Ribh, Yeats is obviously able to transpose this understanding of the bisexual God into the terms of an approach to the internal deity of the Self. In his essay 'The Mandukya Upanishad' he wrote:

> An Indian devotee may recognise that he approaches the Self through the transfiguration of sexual desire; he repeats thousands of times a day words of adoration, calls before his eyes a thousand times the divine image. He is not always solitary, there is another method, that of the Tantric philosophy, where a man and woman, when in sexual union, transfigure each other's images into the masculine and feminine characters of God.

In the third stanza the argument of the poem emerges. Since 'all must copy copies, all increase their kind,' how can God as the source of all be entirely masculine as in the Christian Trinity? The resolution of 'Ribh denounces Patrick', in its fourth and last stanza, is by way of the Vedantic doctrine of the active, self-begetting principle of the Universe: male *purusha* (spirit) in union with female *prakriti* (matter) as forming the two poles of all manifestation:

The mirror-scalèd serpent is multiplicity,
But all that run in couples, on earth, in flood or air, share
   God that is but three,
And could beget or bear themselves could they but love as He.

The doctrine of God as masculine cosmic seed and feminine cosmic matrix as paradigm of the types of Love, used with such deftness of touch and such profound insight here, suggests not only the common divinity of man and all created couples, but also the necessity of their begetting endlessly that multiplicity of all things until, in perfect love (enlightenment in Supreme Self), the completeness of their love transforms all generative process into the Unity of the One Being. Yeats thought the point of the poem, so he confessed in a letter to Mrs. Shakespeare, was that 'we beget and bear because of the incompleteness of our love'. He had already written in the revised A Vision: 'the natural union of man and woman has a kind of sacredness . . . I see in it a symbol of that eternal instant where the antinomy is resolved.'

The next poem, 'Ribh in Ecstasy', develops quite naturally out of its predecessor. It is built around the idea of the attained moment of Unity as the soul unites in 'sexual spasm' with its own 'cause or ground'. The male/female configuration is here extended to the level of the soul's act of enlightenment:

> My soul has found
> All happiness in its own cause or ground.
> Godhead on Godhead in sexual spasm begot
> Godhead.

'Those amorous cries that out of quiet come' are analogously the cosmic act of sexuality. Ribh, the ascetic figure of the saint, in the act of self-communion, has gone to the 'centre' to identify himself, completely and without the intermediacy of any form whatever, with the ground of all existence. This is the third stage of the Yogi's concentration described in both *Aphorisms of Yoga* (translated by the Swami), and by Yeats in his Introduction to *The Holy Mountain*:

> The third stage is *Sushupti*, a complete disappearance of all but this identity. Nothing exists but that . . . majesty, that beauty; the man has disappeared as the sculptor in his statue, the musician in his music. One remembers the Japanese philosopher's saying, 'What the artist perceives through a medium, the saint perceives immediately.'

It is not until the fourth stage of concentration that the ascetic has the ability to hold this condition at will. Even so the 'shadow' in the following lines is the darkness of the causal body of existence that breaks in upon the ascetic's moment of inner illumination. It is the soul's attachment to the individual self that loosens Ribh's grasp of his ultimate identity with the Supreme.

> Some shadow fell. My soul forgot
> Those amorous cries that out of quiet come
> And must the common round of day resume.

The four lines that comprise 'There' demonstrate by their richness of allusion Yeats's vast store of imaginative thought.

> There all the barrel-hoops are knit,
> There all the serpent-tails are bit,
> There all the gyres converge in one,
> There all the planets drop in the Sun.

At their simplest these lines may be said to describe the moment of Supreme Identity become transparent to its cosmic dimensions. The metaphysical locus of the poem is the fourth stage of Yogic concentration, which Yeats describes in his Introduction to *The Holy Mountain*:

In the fourth stage the ascetic enters one or more of these stages at will and retains his complete memory when he returns; this . . . *Turiyā* or seedless *Samādhi* comes when all [the previous] states are as a single timeless act, and that act is pure or unimpeded personality, all existence brought into the words: 'I am'. It resembles that last Greek number, a multiple of all numbers because there is nothing outside it, nothing to make a new beginning. It is not only seedless but objectless because objects are lost in complete light.

By the terms of the system of *A Vision*, 'There' is the circle become sphere:

The whole system is founded upon the belief that the ultimate reality, symbolised as a Sphere, falls in human consciousness, as Nicholas of Cusa was the first to demonstrate, into a series of antinomies . . .. The ultimate reality, because neither one nor many, concord nor discord, is symbolised as a phaseless sphere, but as all things fall into a series of antinomies in human experience it becomes, the moment it is thought of . . . the thirteenth cone . . . that instant of necessity unintelligible to all bound to the antinomies . . . it is in every man and called by every man his freedom.

The reference to de Cusa provides a clue to the symbolism of the poem's first line: 'There all the barrel-hoops are knit.' In his *Vision of God*, de Cusa speaks of God as being 'girt' round by the coincidence of contradictories. God is thus beyond the *coincidentia oppositorum*, the dichotomy between freedom and the determined which reaches from ultimate reality to everyday consciousness, and so 'binds' as well as contains the 'barrel' of His creation.

In the second line, 'There all the serpent-tails are bit', Yeats presents us with a symbol he must have studied in many guises. In the Gnostic tradition of which he was so assiduous a student it is usually coloured half light and half dark, symbolising the opposites—active/passive, affirmative/negative, constructive/destructive, good/evil—that comprise the flux of cyclic manifestation. 'There', in this moving image of the Eternal itself, is where all cosmic process is sustained.

In the third line, 'There all the gyres converge in one', we return to Yeats's system with its interpenetrating gyres symbolising the sexual act that momentarily opens upon the beatific vision, but here on a cosmic scale that allows all the created antinomies of existence their resolution in the identity of the One and the Manifold: at the level of the psyche the unification of soul and daimon, carnal and spiritual self.

The fourth and last line, 'There all the planets drop in the Sun', gives us the archetypal symbol of the cosmic centre itself, the light and 'seat' of all intuitive wisdom, that which illuminates all celestial and all terrestrial reality. It is thus the metaphysical *stasis* from which all life irradiates, the human, civilisational and cosmic cycles prefigured in the movement of the planets, by reflection an expression of the common centre of their orbits. At the moment of Unity all creation drops into the Sun of its own First Cause.

In his Introduction to *Aphorisms of Yoga* Yeats spoke of the moment of Supreme Identity as the central experience of Indian civilisation; 'accessible to all who adopt a traditional technique'. He goes on to consider Goethe's attempt in *Faust* to experience and express such 'a moment acceptable to reason where our thoughts and emotions could find satisfaction or rest'. He concludes:

> If Goethe failed, he failed because neither he nor his audience knew any science or philosophy that sought not a change of opinion, but a different level of consciousness; knowing nothing of white heat he sought truth in the cold iron.

It is in the light of this idea that we can best approach 'Ribh considers Christian Love insufficient', one of the most important of the Supernatural Songs and a central statement of Unity of Being.

The poem is an extended variation, as it were, on a theme that appears in these lines from 'A Prayer for my Daughter':

> Considering that, all hatred driven hence,
> The soul recovers radical innocence
> And learns at last that it is self-delighting,
> Self-appeasing, self-affrighting,
> And that its own sweet will is Heaven's will.

But in the later poem the theme is reworked in terms of the approach of the soul to Ultimate Reality, with Yeats substituting his mask of hatred for the traditional technique of attaining a different level of consciousness. The insufficiency of Christian love for the pre-Christian Ribh lies precisely in the duality of an abstract theology that divides God from Man, Heaven from Earth, Eternity from Time, higher from lower, and denies the correspondence between spirituality and sexuality. It is clear that Yeats had found in his studies with the Swami a 'traditional technique' for the soul's absorption in God that escaped, in his own words, 'mere credulity or religiosity'.

Since love comes unsought from God and hatred from man, Ribh seeks to study only the latter, the better to grasp the roots of the soul's attachment to all 'that is not mind or sense'. But his soul, as 'bride' of God, is jealous of the self's attachment to 'man, woman or event', that same self in which hatred will 'discover impurities'. These impurities are the hindrances that prevent the soul from recognising its true identity in the Supreme Being. In Patanjali's *Aphorisms* they are described so; 'Ignorance, egoism, desire, aversion, fear are afflictions. Ignorance is the cause, the others are the effects, whether they are dormant, weak, suppressed or aggravated'. But, free of the false identification of itself with these modes of the carnal self's ignorance, the soul of Ribh

> can show at last
> How soul may walk when all such things are past,
> How soul could walk before such things began.

That is to say, purged of every sensual attachment by hatred of it, the soul reaches a 'different level of consciousness' of reality, one in which, as a passage in the *Aphorisms* puts it:

> past and future exist as much as present . . . . If the past and future did not exist in reality, the yogi could not have seen them through concentration; he does not create the past, he only sees it as it happened; he does not create the future, he only sees it as it will happen. Man does not see the past as he does not see the part of the road he has travelled, neither does he see the future as he does not see the part of the road he has yet to travel, because of his limited vision.

We have to transpose Ribh's 'hatred of God' as a mode of purification of the self analogous to the Yogi's concentration.

The 'delivered soul', however, learns a 'darker knowledge' which, from an early draft of the poem, we know to be knowledge of good and evil. At its new level of consciousness the soul is no longer subject to good and evil, these being the (last) veil of 'trash and tinsel' that adorn it and so come between the soul and its desire to nakedly embrace God. Even hatred of any remaining conception of God as involved with good and evil (terms of the carnal self's morality, no more) is needed to 'bring the soul to God'.

The 'stroke of midnight' ('that last dark', in an earlier draft) with which the last stanza of the poem opens is the moment of embodiment of Unity of Being in which 'soul cannot endure / A bodily or mental furniture'.

It is also the bride-soul's moment of death in the bosom of God, free of all external and predestined reality and without any intermediate terms of reference. The last four lines make it clear that for the ascetic Ribh the insufficiency of any search or study of moral religiosity or theological dialectic (Yeats tilting at dogma?) is proven by the soul's need to submit completely to God's Will before that Will can be known: the soul, in the Unity of the final illumination (Turiyā) is all that it knows and all that it knows is God.

What can she take until her Master give!
Where can she look until He make the show!
What can she know until he bid her know!
How can she live till in her blood He live!

'He and She', the sixth of the Supernatural Songs, takes as its theme this absorption of the soul in God and plays upon the symbolism of God ('His light') as the groom and the soul ('sacred moon') as His bride. The soul, by rejecting all that is not of its divine essence, in its approach to God ('the further that I fly'), mirrors nothing but His light. But in daring not to stop in her approach she becomes wholly absorbed in God so that in answer to the Supreme (Brahma's) question, 'Who are you?', she answers 'Yourself'—she is free in her identity with the source of all things to claim

'I am I, am I:
The greater grows my light
The further that I fly'.
All creation shivers
With that sweet cry.

As the creator is reflected in his creation, as God is mirrored in the soul, both, like bride and bridegroom, are One in eternal generation at the moment of Unity.

The same question and answer make an oblique contribution to 'Meru', the twelfth and last song of the series; and again we find Yeats juxtaposing East and West. It is obvious from a passage in his essay 'The Holy Mountain' that Meru is symbolic of *Samādhi* ('I find my imagination setting in one line *Turiyā*—full moon mirror-like bright water, Mount Meru), the single timeless act of the words "I am".' In Indian symbolism Meru is the Cosmic Mountain, the central axis uniting Heaven and Earth from which the 'manifold illusion' of the poem is ordered into existence. Not only man in successive incarnations 'century after century', but the successive ordering (after an imaginative pattern) of the human world itself in the civilisations of East and West; as day and night; as man's 'glory and his monuments'; all these fruits of action are sustained in cyclic revolution about a pure being at their centre that is the still and uninvolved witness of their constant flux. The civilisation that is heir to Egypt, Greece and Rome, with its approach to truth through abstraction, is contrasted with that of Asia, which Yeats always thought at its best in its 'care for the spontaneity of the soul'. The one achieves a reality of desolation by its attachment to the fruits of action, while the other, as is implied by the caverned ascetics of the poem, provides Unity of Being—*Turiyā*. Yeats speaks of such hermits (ancestors of Ribh?) in 'The Holy Mountain' as those who, in answering Brahma's question 'Who are you?' with 'Yourself' 'pass out of those three penitential circles, that of common man, that of gifted man, that of the Gods, and find some cavern upon Meru, and so pass out of all life.' It should be remembered that the *axis mundi* is the passage that links all levels of being. Since Yeats had noted in his Diary of 1930 his belief that the present civilisation had reached its meridian —approaching influx he could only conceive as discord—it seems plausible to suggest that in these poems he is pointing to an alternative to western civilisation's 'dangerous fanaticism'—its submission to the external tyrants of time and matter—until such time as it reaches its term in (as he wrote in his 1930 Diary) a 'Being or an Olympus all can share'.

Looking back over these songs we can recognise them as explorations of the silence that beckoned in the earlier 'Vacillation' (VII).

> *The Soul.* Seek out reality, leave things that seem.
> *The Heart.* What, be a singer born and lack a theme?
> *The Soul.* Isaiah's coal, what more can man desire?
> *The Heart.* Struck dumb in the simplicity of fire!
> *The Soul.* Look on that fire, salvation walks within.
> *The Heart.* What theme had Homer but original sin?

These lines epitomise that war with himself which fed the poet's creative impulse; the contending demands of the inexpressible 'centre' and the heart's passion at the 'rim' of the sensual flux.

While Yeats believed 'passion desires its recurrence more than any other event', the revelatory *stasis* of the saint's absorption in God was necessary to his myth of Unity of Being. Passion may fuel that life of man poets sing, yet it must proceed from and again return to that 'immortal fire'[5] that is the Total Presence within and of which it is an expression. It is Boehme's 'principle of every Life' which, when known, is that by which all things are known. In the words of the Yeats/Swami translation of the *Brihadāranyaka Upanishad*:

> ascetics who know it in solitude, and worship it as faith and truth; pass after death into light, from light into day, from day into the moon's brightning fortnight, from the moon's brightning fortnight into the six months when sun moves northward, from these months into the territory of gods, from the territory of gods into the sun, from the sun into lightning. The self-born Spirit finds them there and leads them to heaven. In that Kingdom of Heaven they live, never returning to earth.

In the ecstatic tensions of the Supernatural Songs, Yeats reached the furthest point of his own spiritual development along the path to Unity via contrariety. Here the antinomy of saint and artist is most nearly resolved in terms of the saint, who, in completing his nature in union with God becomes *absolutely* 'himself'. Yeats's myth of Unity— that the essence of man's humanity is his participation in the Divine, his knowledge of God by way of the inner affinity of God with man —was implicit in the poet's belief from the start. That he glimpsed the possibility of its fullest realisation in his late study of the Vedanta we can hardly doubt. But the uncompounded simplicity, as he recognised, could only be embraced at the price of silence. Some three weeks before his death he wrote to Lady Elizabeth Pelham:

> In two or three weeks ... I will begin to write my most fundamental

thoughts and the arrangement of thought which I am convinced will complete my studies . . .. It seems to me that I have found what I wanted. When I try to put it all into a phrase I say, 'Man can embody truth but he cannot know it.' I must embody it in the completion of my life. The abstract is not life and everywhere draws out in contradiction. You can refute Hegel but not the Saint or the Song of Sixpence.

NOTES

1. W. B. Yeats, *Autobiographies* (London, 1966), p. 255. Yeats abandoned mediumship some years before his death. Kathleen Raine supplies an interesting discussion concerning this in her essay 'Hades Wrapped in Cloud' in *Yeats the Initiate* (London, 1986), pp. 1–32.

2. A possible source for the iconography of the second line of 'Veronica's Napkin' is J. H. Philpot's *The Sacred Tree* (1897): 'According to the Phonecians the universe was framed on the model of a tent, its axis a revolving cosmic tree, supporting a blue canopy on which the heavenly bodies were embodied.'

3. Yeats had two masters from whom he learned the complexities of this traditional cosmic symbol. For Blake it was the very essence of the life-force—'Without contraries is no progression', while for de Cusa it was the gateway to Heaven: 'I begin, Lord, to behold Thee in the door of the coincidence of opposites, which the angel guardeth that is set over the entrance to Paradise'. Nicholas of Cusa, *The Vision of God*, translated by Emma Gurney Salter (London, 1928), p. 46.

4. In 'An Indian Monk' (1932) he wrote: 'Christendom has based itself upon four short books and for long insisted that all must interpret them in the same way. It was at times dangerous for a painter to vary, however slightly, the position of the Nails upon the Cross. The greatest saints have had their books examined by the Holy Office . . ... Since the Renaissance, literature, science, and the fine arts have left the Church and sought elsewhere the variety necessary to their existence.'

5. The importance of the symbol of fire to Unity of Being can be seen from a number of passages, such as this from his *Essays* (1924), in which unity of consciousness is likened to an activity where 'all opposites meet and there only is the extreme of choice possible, full freedom. And there the heterogeneous is, and evil, for evil is the strain one upon another of opposites; but in the condition of fire is all music and all rest.' That same 'fire' is the provenance of 'the flame that cannot singe a sleeve' in 'Byzantium': it is the Heraclitian 'fire of heaven' in which all things are consumed', the intangible activity of the splendour of Being itself, 'the fire where all the Universe "returns to its seed".' See section VI of 'The Great Year of the Ancients' in *A Vision*. See also *Essays and Introductions*, pp. 440-41 and *Explorations*, pp. 324-25.

Yourself, the Finder Found

Leave us this residue, this virgin ground
For ever fresh

'Time Held in Time's Despite'

THE POETRY OF EDWIN MUIR IS PRE-EMINENTLY ONE OF A
spiritual nostalgia which looks back to the pre-fall image of man at the
same time as it looks forward to the possible re-sacralisation of this
world. In postulating the lost yet still implicit spiritual goal mysteri-
ously present at the heart of our temporal experience, Muir expresses
that characteristic of man that makes him an exile in this world. It is a
poetry centred on the loss of the knowledge of what man really *is* that is
at the same time the remembrance of what is intrinsic to his ultimate
destiny. This nostalgia is nothing less than the intuition of the lost
Paradise within—the divine source and centre of man's being without
which he would be quite literally unintelligible. Muir himself wrote;
'human beings are understandable only as immortal spirits'.

This divine ground of the inward Eden is accessible to the extent of
our willingness to penetrate beyond the veil time weaves from contingent realities, so obscuring the contours of the eternal world. In terms
of Muir's poetic vision, man is necessarily attached to the 'great non-
stop heraldic show' of this world that yet hides from him the simple
joy and wholeness of that Eden from whence he came and towards
which his destiny always points him. The poet's vision is rooted in the
discovery of his own spiritual origins. As he wrote in his *Autobiography*,
'In turning my head and looking *against* the direction in which time
was hurrying me I won a new kind of experience . . . I could see life
timelessly . . . in terms of the imagination.' The presiding themes of
Muir's imaginative vision can be traced through the ostensibly per-

sonal, very often confessional, tone of the poems; the necessity for the inward quest to the 'sacred centre', to retrace one's spiritual home—and the journey towards an eternal origin.

These poems elaborate the inward and outward obstacles encountered during the journey, which is an attempt to cheat the determinism of time's forward momentum; the one-dimensional truth and reality it discloses. The poet's vision presents the context of the struggle between the recognition of Grace and his acknowledgement of the necessity of Fate. The tension between these two engenders the vicissitudes of the individual life, which must be shaped against the pattern of Eternal life. For Muir this individual life is 'the Story'; yet in so far as it is prefigured in the Archetype—the life of every man regardless of time or place—it is also 'the Fable'. Each must be understood in terms of the other, and this gives both their meaning. Muir believed that the inner Paradise cannot be known but only glimpsed while man is part of the terrestrial world. In other words, the 'Fable' cannot be fully realised while we are part of the 'Story'. In The Story and the Fable, his first autobiographical volume, he wrote 'what we are not and never can be, our fable, seems to me inconceivably interesting. Though we may know innocence and the Fall yet we must posit the Resurrection.' It would be too simple to say merely that the poems spring from a struggle between the opposing demands of the material and spiritual worlds, for always present in Muir's poetry is that wholeness of vision of the greater mystery that provides the context for their reconciliation.

Characteristically, Muir ends his poem 'The Transfiguration' in this key. Here the poet postulates 'a time when time is ripe', when all men achieve the moment of wholeness, the moment that occasions their unanimous call for Christ whose reappearance transfigures and redeems all history—the temporal veil. At such a moment all human strife and partiality, all cosmic separateness and fragmentation, is plunged into the unity and wholeness whence it arose. But we shall return to this, one of Muir's greatest poems, later.

For the poet, only love can bring about such a total transfiguration of the world of time and space. It is love that acknowledges the immortality of the soul and so provides the necessary condition of imaginative vision. That creative intuition, the source of the truth the heart knows, must be greater than the cumulative, temporal play of history for, as he put it in 'Song' 'love gathers all' disparities and opposites 'to one place at last'. Were it otherwise, all life would seem hopelessly predetermined so that

> Man from himself is led
> Through mazes past recall,
> Distraction can disguise
> The wastrel and the wise
> Till neither knows his state:
> Love gathers all.

For Muir, imagination is common to all men since it is the ability to bring to focus in a particular person or emotion its rootedness in Being itself. Imaginative truth reflects without distortion or depreciation a being's uniqueness as it takes its place in the eternal pattern of all things. In his essay 'A View of Poetry', he wrote:

Imagination unites us with humanity in time and space; by means of it we understand Hector and Achilles in their distant world, and feel the remote emotion in a Chinese poem; in such things we are at one with universal mankind and ourselves. That is the work of the imagination, and our lives would not have any meaning if they were quite without it.

Thus, it is not the factual exactitude of the individual life that is of greatest importance but its relation, however distantly intimated in common experience, to the destiny of the whole man—body, soul and spirit. The supreme expression of imagination, Muir thought, is in poetry in which the common bond that knits together the many lives of men is most intensely realised. Here it is given its most heightened expression in order to move men towards the truth which—because it does not correspond to one specific kind of knowledge, since it is the good of all knowledge—'shall set men free'. It is the very opposite of abstract thought, which emprisons the mind in 'ideas and categories'. Imagination apprehends 'living beings and living creatures as they live and move', the more faithfully to reflect the wellsprings of their eternal and abiding essence.

We have, from Muir, then, a body of poetry whose occasion is the nostalgia of spiritual exile from 'the clear unfallen world' of the interior Eden—the 'lost original of the soul'. It is a poetry that traces, through the imaginative consonance of myth, symbol and emblematic imagery, the timeless pattern underlying the individual's involvement with time as the vehicle of man's destiny on the one hand, and on the other the passage to the eternal reality that redeems time by completing it. Although he began by seeing time as the enemy to be conquered and destroyed, with increasing poetic maturity Muir understood that soul must come to terms with time. As he concludes in 'Day and Night':

> A man now, gone with time so long—
> My youth to myself grown fabulous
> . . .
> I try to fit that world to this,
> The hidden to the visible play,
> Would have them both, would nothing miss.

The poet, through the integrity of his art, pictures the harmony made possible by the influx of Grace into the domain where good and evil, beauty and ugliness, love and strife, faith and betrayal hold sway. The context of these contending forces is expressed, in the poems, in vivid images of things quietly observed and deeply felt. Images of *stasis* of place—the wall, the field, the hill—appear together with images of orientation and quest—the 'turning maze of chance', 'the ever running road', the voyage, and the journey. These are so many obstacles that prevent the soul from knowing that 'radiant kingdom' where all is 'in its proper place'. Such obstacles speak of the soul's attachment to the world wherein man must live out his life but which of itself is seen as an 'insufficient place', always a-making. Even so, acceptance of one's place in the order of one's fate remains fundamental to the poet's vision. The theme is announced early in 'Variations on a Time Theme':

> Alas! no heavenly voice the passing told
> Of that last Eden; my own bliss I sold.
> Weary of being one, myself conspired
> Against myself and into bondage hired
> My mortal birthright . . .
> Set free, or outlawed, now I walk the sand
> And search this rubble for the promised land.

The symbols of Muir's vision characterise the inner laws of his own being that are none the less shared by all men. The imaginative topography of his vision is approached from the viewpoint of the archetypal world. And because his vision rests upon a metaphysical view of the world, the natural order of things and man's response to it are not 'reality' itself but the mediate vehicle for conveying the Real, as we can see in these lines from 'In Love for Long'.

> I've been in love for long
> With what I cannot tell
> And will contrive a song
> For the intangible
> That has no mould or shape,
> From which there's no escape.
>
> It is not even a name,
> Yet is all constancy;
> Tried or untried, the same,
> It cannot part from me;
> A breath, yet as still
> As the established hill.

It is not any thing,
And yet all being is;
Being, being, being,
Its burden and its bliss.
How can I ever prove
What it is I love?

By his consistent attention to the intuition of that intangible and partially hidden world, his continual hold on that constant within his own experience, Muir won an expanding grasp of its interior land-scape. The memory of his simple and direct experiences of childhood —celebrated in 'Childhood', the first of his Collected Poems—became a symbol of the mature man's lost Eden. Of this Eden an over-worldly knowledge is the very destroyer, yet, by way of compensation such knowledge can also prepare us for the task of winning back a measure of that Eden's radiant simplicity. Seen through the vicissitudes of mature experience, as in 'The West', that Paradise is always there, like a calm remembered landscape in summer at the end of the journey, or the labyrinth:

And that great movement like a quiet river,
Which always flowing yet is always the same,
Begets a stillness. So that when we look
Out at our life we see a changeless landscape,
And all disposed there in its due proportion,
The young and old, the good and bad, the wise and foolish,
All these are there as if they had been for ever,
And motionless as statues, prototypes
Set beyond time, for whom the sun stands still.

Late in life, as he records in his *Autobiography*, Muir was able to recognise that two of the three mysteries that possess the human mind are the idea of spiritual origin—'where we come from' and the idea of a sacred centre—'where are we going?'. Thus, in 'The Journey Back', the purpose of the journey is to

Seek the beginnings, learn from whence you came,
And know the various earth of which you are made.

The end of this inner voyage to the sacred centre is seen in 'The Mountains' in terms of a summit

> whose height
> Will show me every hill,
> A single mountain on whose side
> Life blooms for ever and is still.

The journey, which in 'I have been taught', passes through

> the sultry labyrinth
> Where all is bright and the flare
> Consumes and shrivels
> The moist fruit

is undertaken in 'fallen' conditions dictated by time and is hazardous, encompassing, in 'The Recurrence'

> what the eye
> From its tower on the turning field
> Sees and sees and cannot tell why,
> Quarterings on the turning shield,
> The great non-stop heraldic show.

There comes the realisation (in section seven of 'The Journey Back') that the beginning is also the end; for the one who journeys, the journey and the journey's end are one:

> Yet in this journey back
> If I should reach the end, if end there was
> Before the ever-running roads began
> And race and track and runner all were there

> Suddenly, always, the great revolving way
> Deep in its trance;—if there was ever a place
> Where one might say, 'Here is the starting-point,'
> . . .
> If I should reach that place, how could I come
> To where I am but by that deafening road,
> Life-wide, world-wide, by which all come to all,
> . . .
> Borne hither on all and carried hence with all,
> We and the world and that unending thought
> Which has elsewhere its end and is for us
> Begotten in a dream deep in this dream
> Beyond the place of getting and of spending.

The journey through darkness and tribulation that traces the individual life to its source takes in 'ever-running roads' that seem themselves 'a part of the great labyrinth'—that 'endless maze' whose deep centre coincides with our awareness of ourselves at the centre of the itinerant pattern that is our own particular and vulnerable life-maze. Here is the theme in 'The Question':

> Will you, sometime, who have sought so long and seek
> Still in the slowly darkening hunting ground,
> Catch sight some ordinary month or week
> Of that strange quarry you scarcely thought you sought—
> Yourself, the gatherer gathered, the finder found.

The maze or the labyrinth characterise the perplexing inner tensions that arise from the effort of vigilance to steer a path between the entangled demands of the natural man on the one hand and the needs of the spiritual man on the other. Amid the disordered flux and multiplicity of man's appetites and reactions, only that which is free of them can provide the ordered pattern of permanence and truth. For Muir this fitting of 'the hidden to the visible play' is the most compelling need of our common experience. 'Soliloquy' speaks of how striving to master the intricacies of the individual life uncovers its true extent and mystery:

> And so I turn
> To past experience, watch it being shaped,
> But never to its own true shape. However,
> I have fitted this or that into the pattern,
> Caught sight sometimes of the original
> That is myself.

In all the poems there is this underlying pattern, the knowledge that the individual life in some mysterious way bodies forth what is Universal. There is, of course, nothing new in this, except that Muir lends the theme his own authentic colouring. Only the tarnished impurity of the natural world and the ordering radiance of the spiritual world conjoined can form the 'sufficient place' of the drama of man's life. These lines are from the final section of 'The Last War':

> About the well of life where we are made
> Spirits of earth and heaven together lie.
> They do not turn their bright heads at our coming,
> So deep their dream of pure comingled being.

A Christian poet (more 'by convergence of symbol than by subscription to doctrine' as Kathleen Raine has observed), Muir, in 'The Recurrence', saw it as evident vindication of the immutably Real that Christ died on the Cross, for nothing that comes from man himself is able to redeem his fallen condition:

> What is not will surely be
> In the changed unchanging reign,
> Else the Actor on the Tree
> Would loll at ease, miming pain,
> And counterfeit mortality.

From such truth there is no escape since even

> Love's agonies, victory's drums
> Cannot huddle the Cross away.

The themes of Muir's poetry share that complexity all art must have that touches upon the roots of the human mystery. The interpenetration of time with Eternity, the recovery of primordial innocence, the path through the maze; the journey along the road, such themes are repeatedly explored in the light of an ever-deepening experience. In the beautiful poem 'Orpheus' Dream', the soul's journey back to its archetypal Self, symbolised by Orpheus' journey, is seen in terms of the Platonic *anamnesis*:

> As if we had left earth's frontier wood
> Long since and from this sea had won
> The lost original of the soul,
> The moment gave us pure and whole
> Each back to each, and swept us on
> Past every choice to boundless good.

In 'Adam's Dream',

> the first great dream
> Which is the ground of every dream since then,

the journey is envisaged in Biblical terms. Here Muir explores the united themes of the Fall and Time. Adam's state of innocence before the Fall was 'his age long daydream'. After the Fall, no longer innocent, Adam dreams a dream of earthly life as a sequence of meaningless events without order or proportion in the wastes of a desert plane filling

> As by an alien arithmetical magic
> Unknown in Eden, a mechanical

117

Addition without meaning, joining only
Number to number in no mode or order,
Weaving no pattern. For these creatures moved
Towards no fixed mark even when in growing bands
They clashed against each other and clashing fell
In mounds of bodies. For they rose again,
Identical or interchangeable,
And went their way that was not like a way.

Such events, being merely earthly and quantitative, obscure the archetypal realm; individual consciousness of time replaces knowledge of the sacred pattern:

'This is time',
Thought Adam in his dream, and time was strange
To one lately in Eden.

Slowly, the true significance of the Fall dawns upon him—he is overwhelmed by nostalgia, and the growing abyss of duration overrides the timeless moment of joyous unity he has now lost:

Adam longed
For more, not this mere moving pattern, not
This illustrated storybook of mankind
Always a-making, improvised on nothing.

He recognises in the faces of the people who begin to inhabit the plain that they too share his 'fallen' condition—are in fact himself.

At that he was among them, and saw each face
Was like his face, so that he would have hailed them
As sons of God but that something restrained him.
And he remembered all, Eden, the Fall,
The Promise, and his place, and took their hands

That were his hands, his and his children's hands,
Cried out and was at peace, and turned again
In love and grief in Eve's encircling arms.

In the grief of his now less than divine state, his 'human' love for Eve
is all that is left to remind him, like some impoverished reflection, of
his former state of love in God before this his first dream—for the
dream and the Fall are one.

The nostalgia that pervades these poems fuels the incentive to man's
abiding vocation (in the original sense of a divine call) to rediscover
one's divine image. We recall the words of Basil of Cæsarea, 'The
human being is an animal who has received the vocation to become
God.' That is, to do the work appointed by one's own proper nature of
realising its intrinsic end in the original ground of Being itself. For
Muir that is the purpose of the journey through the Maze or along the
'ever-winding' road that is the momentum of the temporal order of
things. Only in our acceptance of the perplexities of the journey, as in
the earlier 'The Road', is that relentless order of things redeemed, for

> There the beginning finds the end
> Before beginnings ever can be,
> And the great runner never leaves
> The starting and the finishing tree,
> The budding and the fading tree.

With each soul undertaking the journey for itself, the task presents
itself ever anew, as in 'The Succession':

> We through the generations came
> Here by a way we do not know
> From the fields of Abraham,
> And still the road is scarce begun.
> To hazard and to danger go
> The sallying generations all
> Where the imperial highways run.

Such beliefs were to the poet intimations of the norm of human existence. They are, as he wrote in his *Autobiography*,

> natural to man for they satisfy his mind and heart better than any alternative ones. The mark of such beliefs is their completeness; they close the circle. In a state of irremediable imperfection such as man's the circle can be closed only by calling on something beyond man; by postulating a transcendent reality. So the belief in eternity is natural to man; and all the arts, all the forms of imaginative literature, since they depend of that belief, are equally natural to him.

This naturalness is abundantly evident in the poems where, for instance, he chooses the animal kingdom (at times it comprises the actual beasts of his childhood Orkney fields; at other times they are heraldic animals) to elaborate his theme. What metaphysical poet could fail to see that the whole of the animal kingdom of which man is part has its necessary role to play in the total harmony of the Creation. According to Genesis the animal kingdom was created before Man and so does not partake of the Fall to the extent that Man himself does. Because of their greater innocence, the creatures signify embodiments of the celestial world. (The whole of 'The Animals' exemplifies Muir's understanding of the relation between man and the animal kingdom.) Thus, even the man who has banished angels from the realm of his imagination has always before him in the animals living evidence of the celestial worlds' influx into terrestrial life:

> as if they had been sent
> By an old command to find our whereabouts
> And that long-lost archaic companionship.
> . . .
> Dropped in some wilderness of the broken world,
> Yet new as if they had come from their own Eden.

That is how the poet speaks of them—'their coming our beginning' —in one of his greatest 'animal' poems 'The Horses'.

In another and very different poem, 'The Late Swallow', the swallow is urged, in the face of the oncoming darkness, to return to that 'radiant tree' whose source of light it had earlier announced; for the age, like the 'narrowing day', is coming to an end for want of its all-informing luminescence:

> Leave, leave your well-loved nest,
> Late swallow, and fly away.
> Here is no rest
> For hollowing heart and wearying wing.
> . . .
> Shake out your pinions long untried
> That now must bear you there where you would be
> Through all the heavens of ice;
> Till falling down the homing air
> You light and perch upon the radiant tree.

In the earlier poems, animals are represented at the level of simple reminiscence, as no more than components of the landscape that contains them. In the later poems they possess much deeper resonances, being clearly emblematic of those instincts that link man both to a pattern of existence in harmony with the world of nature, and to the world of celestial light.

In the closing lines of 'Dialogue' ('I never saw the world') the emblematic steed of fabulous origin, 'the high horse glorified', is contrasted with the more brotherly beast that 'must answer/To bit and rein' and whose work is the patient cultivation of fields:

> I have known men and horses many a day.
> Men come and go, the wise and the fanciful.
> I ride my horse and make it go my way.

121

Both kinds of horses seem united in 'Sunset' where, in a landscape that reminds us of the Elysian fields within us whose patient cultivation is man's primordial task, the horse is transmuted through 'bodiless fire' to become a vestige of the sacred in the 'half-heaven' of that 'evening world' on which the sun is setting:

> now each bush and tree
> Stands still within the fire,
> And the bird sits on the tree.
> Three horses in a field
> That yesterday ran wild
> Are bridled and reined by light
> As in a heavenly field.
> Man, beast and tree in fire,
> The bright cloud showering peace.

Are not such horses also distant cousins of the pair of winged steeds to which Plato likened the human soul—higher emotions and bodily cravings that must be brought into harmony with each other?

The spiritual orientation of Muir's poetry moves from darkness into light—from memories of his childhood, with its betrayal by 'unpitying Time', through the dream symbols of his psychoanalysis ('glints of immortality'), to his possession of that transcendent kingdom where he had, as he confesses in 'Soliloquy',

> followed Plato to eternity,
> Walked in his radiant world.

This 'radiant world' is envisaged throughout the poems as an amalgam of the Biblical and Platonic worlds with the mythological world of the Greek Heroes.

In 'Prometheus', for instance, Muir, in characteristic fashion, portrays the Hero as a type of Man: the Forethinker. Early in the poem Muir's basic motif of man's spiritual pilgrimage to the end, which is also his beginning (the 'road' on which all men inescapably, if variously, find themselves), is again suffused with Platonic recollection:

> pilgrim man
> Travels foreknowing to his stopping place,
> Awareness of his lips, which have tasted sorrow
> Foretasted death.

The Hero, chained and suffering on the rock, from the perspective of his time-bound fate, considers the earth-bound race of God-less men:

> These strangers do not know
> Their happiness is in that which leads their sorrow
> Round to an end.

Whereas Prometheus prays for a redeeming end to time, these 'sons of man' hope only for an escape from it, living as they do in

> Lands without gods; nothing but earth and water;
> Words without mystery; and the only creed
> An iron text to beat the round skulls flat
> And fit them for the cap of a buried master.

But the poet visualises the day of 'the world's end' as one in which Christ alone will 'hear and answer' the tale he could tell of man's rejection of the Divine and his attempt to live in the single dimension of the temporal and the material, so that by 'time's storm rising' he is swept

> into an emptier room,
> Vast as a continent, bare as a desert
> Where the dust takes man's lifetime to revolve
> Around the walls, harried by peevish gusts
> And little spiteful eddies; nothing standing
> But the cast-iron cities and rubbish mountains.

At the last, the rebellious Greek God becomes a spokesman for the Christian Redemption of time by Him who

> came down, they say, from another heaven
> Not in rebellion but in pity and love,
> Was born a son of a woman, lived and died,
> And rose again with all the spoils of time
> Back to his home, where now they are transmuted
> Into bright toys and various frames of glory;
> And time itself is there a world of marvels.

This specifically Christian vision of the redemption of time serves to gather and clarify with renewed vigour the metaphysical and spiritual implications of Muir's later poetry. His sustained intuition of the 'clear unfallen world' constantly spills over into his vision of the natural world, so that the mundane is itself transfigured.

This is the point of departure of 'The Transfiguration', where the fusion of the one world with the other takes place so quietly and naturally it is as if the Divine were suddenly and effortlessly apparent to everyday consciousness, completing it by bathing it in its transcendent source:

> So from the ground we felt that virtue branch
> Through all our veins till we were whole, our wrists
> As fresh and pure as water from a well,
> Our hands made new to handle holy things,
> The source of all our seeing rinsed and cleansed
> Till earth and light and water entering there
> Gave back to us the clear unfallen world.
> We would have thrown our clothes away for lightness,
> But that even they, though sour and travel stained
> Seemed, like our flesh, made of immortal substance.

'Was it a vision?' the poet asks,

Or did we see that day the unseeable
One glory of the everlasting world
Perpetually at work, though never seen
Since Eden locked the gate that's everywhere
And nowhere?

In this, one of his finest poems, Muir builds upon only the implied presence of that which is fundamental to his whole vision—that intangible core, the still moment uninvolved in events, the manifest source of all things, intuited by the non-discursive essence of mind. The centre that is *in* but not *of* this world, being (as he wrote in the earlier 'The Original Place')

A stronghold never taken,
Stormed at hourly in vain,
Held by a force unknown
That neither answers nor yields.

To see the world from the perspective of this radiant core reveals not only the latent, numinous essence of things but also a translucence in which all earthly defects can be reconciled to a primordial adequacy:

The painted animals
Assembled there in gentle congregations
Or sought apart their leafy oratories,
Or walked in peace, the wild and tame together,
As if, also for them, the day had come.
The shepherds' hovels shone, for underneath
The soot we saw the stone clean at the heart
As on the starting day. The refuse heaps
Were grained with that fine dust that made the world.

Moreover, it is He who had said, 'To the pure all things are pure'— Christ the Redeemer, who 'will come again', 'at a time when time is ripe', when all the possibilities of the fallen world have come to their final fruition and are exhausted. As the promised fulfilment and Saviour of all that is fallen, the Incarnation of the source of all that suffers, is disfigured, is partial, is subject to death, His return will signal the perpetual restoration of all these things to the innocence and simplicity of their original condition:

> Then he will come, Christ the uncrucified,
> Christ the discrucified, his death undone,
> His agony unmade, his cross dismantled—
> Glad to be so—and the tormented wood
> Will cure its hurt and grow into a tree
> In a green springing corner of young Eden.
> And Judas damned take his long journey backward
> From darkness into light and be a child
> Beside his mother's knee, and the betrayal
> Be quite undone and never more be done.

That same mystery of things in their primordial simplicity informs 'The Sufficient Place' where

> all the silver roads wind in, lead in
> To this still place

that faithfully reflects the archetypal condition at the heart of both inner and outer worlds and is 'sufficient' in that it corresponds to the ultimate need of man's soul:

> Two figures, Man and Woman, simple and clear
> As a child's first images. Their manners are
> Such as were known before the earliest fashion
> Taught the Heavens guile. The room inside is like
> A thought that needed thus much space to write on,
> Thus much and no more. Here all's sufficient. None
> That comes complains, and all the world comes here,

Comes, and goes out again, and comes again.
This is the Pattern, these the Archetypes,
Sufficient, strong, and peaceful.

Of such truths no argument can ever convince, for he who has not seen cannot bear witness, as these lines from 'The Labyrinth' testify:

That was the real world; I have touched it once,
And now shall know it always. But the lie,
The maze, the wild-wood waste of falsehood, roads
That run and run and never reach an end,
Embowered in error—I'd be prisoned there
But that my soul has bird wings to fly free.

In his *Autobiography* Muir speaks of how he came to realise that he shared with Traherne a common belief that childhood and immortality are bound together. And turning to the seventeenth-century mystic, we discover a passage in his *Third Century* that would seem to refer directly to the Scotsman's vision of that Eden towards which he was, perforce, like us all, constantly to struggle:

Those pure and Virgin Apprehensions I had from the Womb, and in that Divine Light wherein I was born, are the Best unto this day, wherein I can see the Universe. By the Gift of GOD they attended me into the world, and by His special favour I remember them till now. Verily they seem the Greatest Gifts His Wisdom could bestow, for without them all other Gifts had been Dead and Vain. They are unattainable by Book, and therefore I will teach them by Experience. Pray for them earnestly; for they will make you Angelical, and wholly Celestial. Certainly Adam in Paradise had not more sweet and Curious Apprehensions of the World, than I when I was a child . . . I knew by Intuition those things which since my Apostasie, I Collected again . . . I seemed as one Brought into the Estate of Innocence . . . I saw all the Peace of Eden; Heaven and Earth did sing my Creators' Praises . . . Is it not strange, that an infant should be heir of the whole World . . . but all things abided eternally as they were in their proper places . . . so that with much ado I was corrupted and made to learn the dirty devises of this world. Which now I unlearn, and become, as it were, a little child again that I may enter into the Kingdom of God.

In Muir's poetry each word acts as a support and pointer towards an essential motif that is never fully explored in any one poem. As we might expect from a poet of comprehensive vision, each poem presents another dimension of the whole of which it is a part. Such is their imaginative integrity that no single poem can be fathomed fully for its richness of resonance and allusion apart from that whole which is all the poems; theme, image and symbol often overlap from poem to poem. Their strength lies in the undeviating resolve of their mutual direction. Muir's vision gives back to us a dimension of our being that life all too readily wrests from us. Yet for all that we feel a sense of familiarity with the world his vision discloses. It is precisely through the everyday occurrence, the familiar thing, the immediate solution, that one must pass in order to 'thread the labyrinthine way' of one's own spiritual awakening and destiny. As he put it in 'The Emblem':

> I who so carefully keep in such repair
> The six-inch king and the toy treasury,
> Prince, poet, realm shrivelled in time's black air,
> I am not, although I seem, an antiquary.
> For that scant-acre kingdom is not dead,
> Nor save in seeming shrunk. When at its gate,
> Which you pass daily, you incline your head,
> And enter (do not knock; it keeps no state)
>
> You will be with space and order magistral,
> And that contracted world so vast will grow
> That this will seem a little tangled field.

For you will be in very truth with all
In their due place and honour, row on row.
For this I read the emblem on the shield.

Time's Glass Breaks

Man, though fallen, has this strong *Sensibility* and reaching Desire after all the *Beauties*, that can be picked up in fallen Nature. Had not this been the Case, had not *Beauty* and Light, and the *Glory* of Brightness been his first *State* by *Creation*, he would now no more want the Beauty of Objects, than the *Ox* wants to have his Pasture enclosed with beautiful Walls, and painted Gates.

William Law

I am entirely concerned with metaphysical truth.

Vernon Watkins

HERE, THE READER HAD BEST RESPECT THE POET'S CONFESSION, for the poetry of Vernon Watkins, like that of his mentors Dante, Blake, Shelley, Hölderlin and Yeats among them, is best understood in the context of that analogical wisdom which has always conceived the nature and destiny of man as recapitulating within his being the unity of material and spiritual worlds. Watkins's ability to visualise what from the viewpoint of common experience is paradoxical but to intuitive perception becomes transparently clear, stems directly from the 'revolution of sensibility' he underwent as a young man. The change was irreversible and he found himself unable ever again to write from the perspective of time. From the viewpoint of his altered sensibility, the poet gives an unequivocal acknowledgement of the transient nature of knowledge derived from sensory experience alone. These are poems whose central theme is the metaphysics of vision.

From the outset we must acknowledge that the world of temporal duration and of sensible appearances is, in terms of Watkins's poetry, to be 'conquered', if we are to understand the nature of the poet's constantly implied assertion that the natural world is not the ultimate reality. This does not mean that the poetry reduces the objects of sensory experience to mere epiphenomena. What is in question here is clearly the ontological significance of the materially real. Watkins's view presupposes that the apprehension of reality possesses a degree less certitude to the extent that it is removed from ultimate reality itself. The 'material shell' (the spectrum or 'music of colours') is the extreme reflexive limit of that which is only perceived in the direct immediacy of imaginative intuition.

To move in apprehension from sensory experience towards increasingly immaterial levels of reality, perception itself must be appropriate to the level of reality so perceived. Watkins's use of the symbolism of light, stream, fire, fountain and music implicitly claims the ontological act of poetic imagination as the means by which man is able to perceive the interpenetration of levels of reality, and presupposes that the qualitative essences of things may be expressed in a language of analogy based on images of nature. There is no real ambivalence involved in Watkins's view that all transience is an 'illusion', for while it has being in a moment of time, it is, as a manifestation of the Divine Principle, never lost to the eternal order of things. Aspects of this perspective are tacitly present in nearly all of the poems from first to last. The late sonnet 'Candle Constant' perfectly concentrates the theme into a single poem:

> This man perceived that time could never catch
> The candle, where it flickered and declined.
> Each flying thought a second thought would snatch,
> Leaving the outline of the first behind;
> A certain aura from a blown-out match
> Was lost, then re-established in the mind.
> What, then, was constant? Still, beyond all doubt,
> All flames were gathered where the last burnt out.

True for him also, certain notes would stay,
The meaning of their own supreme desire
Established perfect where they died away.
Such music, not unlike that constant fire,
Made Earth, as though a fountain were to play,
Fresh for a thousand seasons, night and day.

Here, the permanence of the Eternal is glimpsed in and through the
fluid web of individual impressions registered by the discursive mind,
the continuity of whose apprehensions remains paradoxical since, considered analytically, that continuity is subject to the dying and renewal
of each moment of time. Thus the relation between perceiver and perceived, at the level of discursive cognition, can never be immutable.
Watkins is employing here the law of analogy that sees reflected in
the most transient of objects the very archetype of Beauty itself. The
poet explores the motif of flux embodying 'constancy' in 'The Replica'
where the waterfall, as a symbol of ontological renewal, creates

a perpetual music, and gives light
In fading always from the measuring mind.

In 'Candle Constant', however, the symbol of renewal is only tacitly
present. The act of poetic vision itself is the intuitive agent of that
immanent and inexhaustible spirit of being 'established perfect' in the
seeming continuity of those individual, fleeting impressions. Only in
the intuitive act of imagination is the consubstantiality of 'candle
light' and archetypal fire ('all flames') guaranteed, for there it is the
constant witness of every perception despite all igneous flames having
been extinguished. The recurrent symbol of fire—it is the informing
principle elsewhere, for instance, in 'Earth and Fire' and 'Unity of the
Stream'—in relation to the notion of intuitive perception is important,
being central to Watkins's vision where, as traditionally, it is indicative
of the one substance that is alike the soul's intelligence and the intellect of divine origin that is cosmic activity. The poet's 'constant fire' is

none other than the immediate 'fiery Breath of the Total Presence within us' (Coomaraswamy).

As is so often the case there is a cosmological principle involved in a central belief of the poet's that nothing of the generated world is created in vain. The Infinite Essence, in the process of its manifestation from essence to substance, could not give rise to anything superfluous, since its progressive exteriorisation of Itself is none other than a 'descent' from principial perfection. Since the material world is the extreme limit of this process, its phenomena represent the objective reflection of the Essence, while the underlying coherence of phenomena is the immediate symbol of the Divine Principle. That which explains Plato's view of the world as the fairest of creations also explains the profound reverence accorded to the minute particulars in Watkins's vision. If in their negative aspect the transient nature of appearances makes them illusory, then in their positive aspect—the permanence of their essence—they are the divine 'art'. The abiding reality of appearances is not at their surface but in their interior depth so that they function as symbols when considered from the viewpoint of their qualitative essences. For Watkins, the natural law of decay and regeneration in nature becomes, on the level of intuitive perception, the mirror-image of eternal renewal itself. The poet conveys a sense of the beauties of a natural scene as the magical 'play' of Cosmic Power, all the more tellingly perhaps for its being informed by his belief in the power of art itself, to hold sway over the soul as mediator of the Eternal.

To illustrate both these aspects of his vision one might turn to his poem 'The Immortal in Nature'. The creative tension engendered by the shining of the transcendent in and through the mundane levels of reality is further elaborated in the fourth stanza with the motif of the office of kingship, which, we recall, is the *perpetual* source of temporal power reflecting spiritual authority regardless of the individual human occupant of the office:

> I must forget these things, and yet lose none.
> Music is light, and shadows all are they.

White is the fountain that begot the sun.
Light on the petal falls; then falls the may.

Sometimes the vulture sees his carrion
A speck on Ganges. White on Himalay
The snows ascend above the light of dawn.
Though distance calls us like a clarion,
How ancient is the voice our souls obey.

I tell my soul: Although they be withdrawn,
Meditate on those lovers. Think of Donne
Who could contract all ages to one day,
Knowing they were but copies of that one:
The first being true, then none can pass away.

Where time is not, all nature is undone,
For nature grows in grandeur of decay.
These royal colours that the leaves put on
Mark the year living in its kingly way;
Yet, when he dies, not he but time is gone.

Beethoven's music nature could not stun.
Light rushed from Milton.
                                See the Sistine ray.
There burns the form eternally begun.
That soul whose very hand made marble pray,
The untempted, mightiest master, holds in sway
The wrestling sinews death had seemed to own
And might have owned, but that they were not clay.

In 'Muse, Poet and Fountain' Watkins suggests that the poet himself, in the act of imaginative perception, is capable of overcoming the
destructive, sorrowing experience of the creation's passing and decay
in his ability to reconcile the discordancies and the contrarieties
through the abiding focal point of Eternity:

Though time still falls from future into past,
Nothing is gone my hand may not restore.
Mine is the pulse that makes your pulse beat fast,
Harmonious joy with stillness at the core.

Again, in 'Demands of the Muse' we find these lines—

Born into time of love's perceptions, he
Is not of time. The acts of time to him
Are marginal. From the first hour he knows me
Until the last, he shall divine my words.
In his solitude he hears another.

which reiterate the same motif but in terms approaching Blake's
'Eternity is in love with the productions of time.' The poet speaks
from the perspective of imaginative intuition in the guise of the poet's
Muse who possesses the knowledge that enables Her to see all time in
its simultaneity, in a single act of cognitive apprehension, for 'Vision
makes wise at once'.

This viewpoint of the transcendent 'witness of consciousness' it is the
labour of the poet's craft to embody; labours which, as the related
poem, 'Demands of the Poet', tells us

bring the authentic tears
Which recognise the moment without age.

If man did not possess in the incorruptible core of his soul that for
which he continually thirsts, a faculty that permits him, in moments of
visionary perception, to see beyond the limits of his individual consciousness to a domain of greater permanence and certainty, then
the loss and suffering, the degeneracy that is so indissolubly a part of
'time's wrong' could never be redeemed. Indeed, even life and death in

such circumstances would lose their meaning since only by that which transcends time can time be measured: only by that which remains unaffected by 'living' can the meaning of life be fathomed. To such a viewpoint the poems often signal their commitment, as in this middle section of 'Green Names, Green Moss':

> Swing, life-leaping bell;
> Strike, in the mourning trees.
> No ravisher can tell
> Their secret histories;
> Not one can you reclaim,
> But side-track their loss
> Until the last, loved name
> Is covered with moss,
> Yet every moment must,
> Each turn of head or hand,
> Though disfigured by dust,
> Incorruptibly stand;
> If they are nothing now
> Then they were nothing then.
> Blinded with thirst I know,
> Beneath my foot lie men
> Each laid in his own caul
> Too intricately still
> In the rock of his soul
> Where the pure fountains fill,
> Too sacred to be touched
> By memory or bell.

The inescapability of our sensory involvement in generated existence necessarily directs our perceptions towards that which by its very nature is limited and contingent. But these very limitations are, as it were, the stage on which the interplay between the eternal and the actual worlds is enacted. In Watkins's view the specific function of the poetic vocation is to effect a redemption of this divisive and incomplete mode of perception. The subtle, all-pervasive presence of this theme is present in many of the poems. One such is 'Poets, In Whom Truth Lives', where it becomes the polarising core of a lyricism of exceptional delicacy, illustrated here by these, the first and last two stanzas.

> Poets, in whom truth lives
> Until you say you know,
> Gone are the birds; the leaves
> Drop, drift away, and snow
> Surrounds you where you sing,
> A silent ring.
> . . .
> The abounding river stops.
> Time in a flash grows less
> True than these glittering drops
> Caught on a thread of glass
> Two frosty branches bear
> In trance-like air.
>
> Stoop; for the hollow ground
> Integrity yet keeps
> True as a viol's sound
> Though the musician sleeps.
> Strong is your trust; then wait:
> Your King comes late.

Here, moreover, we find a further extension to a belief of Watkins's poetic faith that the intricate craft of poetry alone gives the true measure to ecstatic vision.[1] The most recurrent motifs that elaborate this theme are those of light and time, whose symbolic ramifications most directly impinge upon the metaphysics of his poetic vision. An exploration of these will clarify by association much else in the poetry.

Light and time only reveal the richness of their full meaning when they are considered as referring to the 'indefinite' extension of space as a symbol of the 'infinite' nature of Being. Height and depth take on a spiritual and metaphysical significance once it is realised that they are symbolic references to the hierarchical structure of Being. Light is synonymous with the source or centre of cosmic manifestation. Being at the highest level qualitatively, it 'falls' by degrees into the existential world of the creature where it is recognised as the condition of corporeal vision. Time, likewise, is the 'fall' of Eternity and is the very condition of the creature's experience of phenomenal reality. Spiritually, both light and time are modes of the descent of the Spirit into the world of nature. In metaphysical terms they represent the manifestation of the Divine Principle reverberating at the material limit of its power and influence. This limit, seen in terms of a sphere, is at the circumference and is thus furthest from the centre or point of origin in Unity and Oneness. It is the plane of utmost differentiation and multiplicity, the natural habitat of, in Watkins's words, man who is 'made of clay'. In the poems, time is co-extensive with and interdependent upon its apprehension by what the poet terms the 'shadow' of individualised consciousness. Manifest light is the image of that immanent Spirit whose illumination is eclipsed by 'shadow'. Light, the 'white light' of the poems, is at the heart of all particular things as a manifestation of their impalpable, eternal essence. It is the 'shadow' of sensory perception that veils the Divine radiance and transparency of things. In the series of Music of Colours poems we can most easily recognise the embodiment and poetic elaboration of these analogical terms of reference.

And yet simply to equate Watkins's symbol of light with Divine Intelligence would do less than justice to the contextual variety of the symbolism in the poems themselves. The appearance of the motifs of 'music', 'white', 'lightning' and 'fountain', for instance, represent various modes of the actualisation of the primal essence of light prior to its refraction into the colours of particularity. None the less, such an equation does provide a definition which satisfies the basic metaphysical significance underlying its imaginative form.

Just how consistent Watkins's use of the light symbol is in this respect, we can discover by turning first to its earliest use in 'Prime Colours' where it appears in conjunction with the fountain motif. Here, Light, being in its origin and potentiality free ('innocent') of any determination, emanates (jets forth) from the primal source, and, like the waters (the inexhaustible potentiality of cosmic possibility) of the Fountain, breaks from a single transparent column into the multiplicity of the colours of the spectrum. The very nature of these qualitative essences, by their brilliance and variegation, 'replicate' the beauty of the Divine Love for its Creation. There is an additional symbolic resonance in the poem that invokes those doctrines that speak of the Creation itself as the primordial act of the Divine Mercy that wanted its Perfection to be known as a reverberation in the imperfection of transient life. The immediately relevant lines of the poem 'Prime Colours' form the poem's final stanza:

> Born of that mud, innocent light he sees,
> The cornerstone in crumbling masonries.
> His washed eyes, marvelling, resurrect the mountain
> Where love's five colours leap into light's fountain.

If we turn to the much later sonnet 'The Measure Moves', light, both inner and outer, is presented through the figure of the blind Samson. In the first stanza the connotations of the symbol are those of the 'immediate fiery breath'—the condition of all apprehension to which mere 'sight' is blind unless 'redeemed' by the vision that acknowledges the celestial origin of every perception. The crucial line is: 'Light is redeemed through eyes which cannot see.' In the last stanza, Samson, time-conscious, blind and bound to the material darkness, invites physical death as a release from his constriction. In so doing, he invokes God to make of his body a receptacle through which may flow, like innumerable arteries of light, the supreme cosmic power and strength—the 'light of life'. The poem ends:

139

Pour light through me, God, through the rivers of my sinew,
And stay me to gather the columns, alive and dead.

A study of the various contexts in which the symbolism of light appears reveals that Watkins envisaged the substance of life as the 'field of manifestation' of the incarnate Spirit. And while nature in particular is the indirect object of its projection, man, in that love and identity with all things which is his theomorphic and primordial perfection, is intrinsically its direct embodiment. In this connection it can be observed that the connotations of the light symbolism tend to polarise into those of spiritual truth, sometimes with Christian, sometimes with pagan and mythic overtones, and those of spiritual beauty, possessing usually Platonic or Neoplatonic overtones. This polarisation reveals the imaginative locus of the poet's sympathies, provided its terms are not pursued to the point of mutual exclusiveness.

For instance, the poem 'Serena' reveals the presence of a 'light of truth' akin to that of the Fourth Gospel. Here, the context of the symbol could hardly fail to remind us of the Gospel's 'light that lighteth every man that cometh into the world'. An infant's birth is envisaged in terms that express its soul as the embodiment of the celestial light of the Divine Intellect or 'First Cause'. The soul ('fallen from light' as the poet wrote in the similar context of 'The Mother and Child' whose terms we can utilize, so consistent are they, to gloss the later poem) is buried in the sensuous darkness of the body ('tomb of each breath') that knows only the corporeal world ('of light in eclipse') where the celestial radiance is lost from immediate view. Traherne spoke of 'The first Light which shined in my Infancy in its primitive and innocent clarity' being 'totally eclipsed' by sensuous knowledge. Here are the first two and the last two stanzas of 'Serena':

> The cradle stirs.
> There life, there innocence, there the miracle shines.
> Old, he is old:
> Life's earliest word, the first. Light has created him
> Out of inscrutable deeps.

And the light breathes;
It breathes in darkness, trembles, trembles and wakes.
There is no help,
There is no help in this room. The divining deluge
Thunders. Time is at hand.

. . .

He will be calm
In the first calm that glittered before knowledge.
Nothing shall change
The Primum Mobile's effectual music
Planted within the breast.

He will be calm,
Not through a reason known to man, nor favour,
But through that gift
The First Cause left, printing upon his forehead
The word 'Serena'.

(The ominous note of the phrase 'time is at hand' is surely the inevitable 'eclipse' by the 'shadow' of individual consciousness that apprehends and is coexistent with temporal duration). The appearance of the light symbol in terms that suggest Platonic connotations inevitably recalls the myth of the Cave as well as the Platonic doctrine of a veiled, divine order of reality against which the world of generated forms seems but a shadowy replica. Here one could point to such poems as 'Foal', 'The Immortal in Nature', 'The Replica', 'Bishopston Stream', the first section of 'Revisited Waters', and, perhaps more characteristically, 'Music of Colours—Dragonfoil and the Furnace of Colours'. In this last poem we find an important allusion to that most central of Platonic doctrines: that the hidden order of reality requires for its apprehension a faculty in comparison with which the state of sensory perception can be likened to a blindness—or partial sleep—the Platonic *anamnesis*.

In the natural world pure Being, symbolised in Watkins's 'white light' or 'fire', the fontal raying of the Divine Principle, is nowhere explicitly evident. Its essence is fragmented into a myriad of contingent aspects known mediately as 'patterns of a lost world' in the objects of sense. Each of these 'shadows of a different order' is a qualitative essence that is connatural with the supra-mental faculty that perceives them. So, analoguously, natural light, 'born of white light,' is connatural with retinal perception to which light always appears mediately as colour. The metaphysical significance of Watkins's 'white light' symbolism, then, provides the focal ambience for an aspect of the poet's imaginative thought that could otherwise be mistakenly interpreted as a somewhat pantheistic view of nature. In 'Music of Colours—Dragonfoil and the Furnace of Colours', the most substantial of the Music of Colours poems, those symbols we have discussed above are interwoven as the very warp and woof of the poem, as these, the last two stanzas, demonstrate:

> Waking entranced, we cannot see that other
> Order of colours moving in the white light.
> Time is for us transfigured into colours
> Known and remembered from an earlier summer,
> Or into breakers.

> Falling on gold sand, bringing all to nothing.
> Fire of the struck brand hides beneath the white spray.
> All life begins there, scattered by the rainbow;
> Yes, and the field flowers, these deceptive blossoms,
> Break from the furnace.

The epiphanic translucence of Watkins's handling of these themes could easily by interpreted in terms of Neoplatonic metaphysical doctrine, provided we guard against the claim that he was a 'Neoplatonic poet' (Plotinus was *one* of the poet's sources). That being said there are certain passages in Plotinus where the ultimate meaning of Watkins's motifs is articulated in a mystical, rather than a poetic context. There is no essential conflict, for instance, between the poet's use of light symbolism as the informing essence of the material world and this passage from the First Ennead—so adequately does it prepare the imaginative ground for the poet's usage:

> The beauty of colour . . . derives . . . from the conquest of the darkness inherent in Matter by the pouring-in of light, the unembodied, which is a Rational-Principle and an Ideal-Form.
>
> Hence it is that Fire itself is splendid beyond all material bodies, holding the rank of Ideal-Principle to the other elements, making ever upwards, the subtlest . . . of all bodies, as very near to the unembodied; itself alone admitting no other, all the others penetrated by it: . . . it has colour primally; they receive the Form of colour from it: hence the splendour of its light, the splendour that belongs to the Idea. And all that has resisted and is but uncertainly held by its light remains outside of beauty, as not having absorbed the plenitude of the Form of colour.[2]

The idea that the light of the corporeal world is the most pleasing and most beautiful of bodies is by no means limited to Greek thought —the universality of the symbol points to its presence as integral to the primordial cosmogonic genesis. Having allowed for the time and place of Watkins's use of this inexhaustible motif, we can see it to be in imaginative consonance with the view of Robert Grosseteste—that perception of light is the greatest of all pleasures since sight is but the harmonious meeting of two types of light, that of the physical world and that of consciousness itself. Boethius held that knowledge of the qualitative essences of things is by their 'form', which is like a light by which we know what things are distinctively. Were it thought that such a consonance did not exist between the poetic vision and the 'unspoken' metaphysics, it would be necessary to claim either that the meaning of the following two stanzas (chosen by way of illustration from 'Music of Colours: The Blossom Scattered') lay in some elaborate and wholly abstract descriptiveness, or that they are devoid of any intelligible content altogether.

So the green Earth if first no colour and then green.
Spirits who walk, who know
All is untouchable, and, knowing this, touch so,
Who know the music by which white is seen,
See the world's colours in flashes come and go.
The marguerite's petal is white, and then is white again
Not from time's course, but from the living spring,
Miraculous whiteness, a petal, a wing,
Like light, like lightning, soft thunder, white as jet,
Ageing on ageless breaths. The ages are not yet.

Is there a tree, a bud, that knows not this:
White breaks from darkness, breaks from such a kiss
No mind can measure? Locked in the branching knot,
Conception shudders; that interior shade
Makes light in darkness, light where light was not;
Then the white petal, of whitest darkness made,
Breaks, and is silent. Immaculate they break,
Consuming vision, blinding eyes awake,
Dazzling the eyes with music, light's unspoken sound,
White born of bride and bridegroom, when they take
Love's path through Hades, engendered of dark ground.

The symbolism of light in Watkins's poetry is best understood in terms of the realisation that non-spatial, non-temporal intuition remains the condition for any interpretation of the terrestrial world. It follows from this that for those 'on whom time's burden falls' the immutably Real is withheld or hidden from common consciousness. Just as the operation rather than the essential nature of retinal perception is by reference to things seen, so we grasp Reality itself only *indirectly* by means of its manifest properties. A discursive knowledge of any thing can only be of its existential nature. Thus, reflected in all created things, as the poet writes in 'The Replica', is 'the image of our life'—that world known to the senses which 'lives by being consumed' and whose

                    countless changes
          Accumulate to nothing but itself.

But when the organ of perception, that 'greatest light' of intuitive vision, purged of all reference to accidents and properties having an anticipated future or remembered past, perceives the 'interval of glory', then all division, particularity and mutability is conquered; then, as the poet put it in 'Great Nights Returning' 'the soul knows the fire that first composed it'.

Here is the theme as it appears at the close of 'The Replica':

                  Yet to man alone,
        Moving in time, birth gives a timeless movement,
        To taste the secret of the honeycomb
        And pluck from night that blessing which outweighs
        All the calamities and griefs of time.
        There shines the one scene worthy of his tears,
        For in that dark the greatest light was born
        Which, if man sees, then time is overthrown,
        And afterwards all acts are qualified
        By knowledge of that interval of glory:
        Music from heaven, the incomparable gift
        Of God to man, in every infant's eyes
        That vision which is ichor to the soul
        Transmitted there by lightning majesty,
        The replica, reborn, of Christian love.

This 'incomparable gift' is part of man's theomorphic nature, so that Eternity is not 'distant' from us though in commonplace experience we are 'far' from It. What needs to be shattered is the illusory 'permanence' that is created by the continuity of the unending series of transient projections which our psycho-physical existence throws upon the screen of consciousness. When 'time's glass breaks', a new reality is not substituted for the familiar one which then becomes somehow impoverished and degraded, but the 'breaking' reveals the transparency of phenomena itself to its luminous source beyond the formal and particular nature of its reflective surface.

Watkins's imagination at all times rests upon this analogical correspondences between, at one level, the eternal world and the spiritual essence of man, and at another, between the external-phenomenal world and man's empirical self. The poet's exploration of these correspondences can be illuminated by reference to the symbolic resonances of metaphysical truth. The symbol of 'Buried Light', for instance, clearly derives its imaginative power from this source. In just the following few lines alone, the ultimate meaning of honour, sublimity, closed eyes, prayer, nobility, sacrifice and mockery would be inexplicable but for the tacit presence of an analogical wisdom capable of seeing the external forms of nature in terms of inner spiritual conditions.

> Come, buried light, and honour time
> With your dear gift, your constancy
> That the known world be made sublime
> Through visions that closed eyelids see.
>
> Come, breath, instruct this angry wind
> To listen here where men have prayed,
> That the bold landscape of the mind
> Fly nobler from its wrist of shade.
>
> Sons of true sacrifice are there.
> Rivers and hills are in their hands.
> The lightest petal the winds bear
> Has mocked the Serpent's swaddling-bands.

This should leave us in no doubt that such correspondences are the integral condition of poetic vision itself.

There is a radical discontinuity between the sensual and sentimental observation of nature and spiritual experience only insofar as our perceptions are confined to the natural order as if it harboured the totality of the Real. And were it not for this discontinuity the natural world would appear to our everyday perceptions as an unending theophany. Watkins gives expression to this dichotomy in the octave of the sonnet 'Two Sources of Life'. The imaginative context of the poem is the flowing river of time beside which stands the Tree of Life. From its branches a man stares at the reflecting surface of the water and is dazzled by the brilliance and vitality of its ever-changing pattern. Yet he is conscious of a deep longing for the need to penetrate beyond this mirrored configuration of the temporal world that so holds him in thrall:

> The time we measure and the time we know
> Move in the branches drinking life, the giver.
> Being young, we bathed here, and shook off the river,
> Then stood above the stream and watched it flow.
> An image in the water shone below,
> Armed with a secret we could not deliver.
> Those beams were like the arrows in a quiver
> For which our expectation was the bow.

The fact that no common measure exists between nature and the Spirit—a fact implicitly acknowledged in the deep thirst man has for an absolute certitude—has its corollary in the doctrine that man must die to his psycho-physical self in order to be reborn in the Spirit. Only in this way can he begin to realise in his soul those possibilities of his nature that are more directly the manifestation of the luminous source of his being and the being of all things. Watkins expresses in the sestet of this sonnet the conjunction of the doctrine of correspondence and the doctrine of self-annihilation. The man, once so impassioned by the strength of his natural perceptions, in maturity suffers a sense of loss of unity and completeness at the experience of death, a suffering that itself enlarges his perceptions and situates them in the perspective of the eternal order which corresponds to that of his soul:

But ask: when was it that the current took us
So deeply into life that time forsook us,
Leaving us nothing but the need to give?
We were transfigured by the deaths of others.
That was the spring, when first we knew our brothers
And died into the truth which made us live.

This deep thirst, then, which is the unresolved accompaniment of all psycho-physical experience, is never at that level alone, satisfied for, if it were, the world of common consciousness would provide every solace and resolve every disequilibrium man ever felt the world had placed upon him. In these lines, from 'The Return of Spring', Watkins can be interpreted as signalling an imaginative empathy with such abiding truths:

And marvellously the sundering, receding seawaves
Pound the resounding sands; they knock at the hour-glass.
Thunder compels no man, yet a thought compels him,
Lost, neglected, yet tender.

Why in the wood, where already the new leaves mending
Winter's wild net, cast fragile, immature shadows,
Do I tread pure darkness, resisting that green dominion?
What is the thing more sacred?

. . .

Once, once only it breaks. If you plunge your fingers
In the stream, all secrets under the Earth grow articulate
In a moment, and for you only.

Diamonds of light, emeralds of leaves, green jewels:
For me the unnoticed, death-touching script is more passionate.
Cover the tome with dust; there dwells the redeemer,
Deathlessly known by the voice-fall.

Only by means of a wisdom that moves 'against times's flow' is the inexorable cycle of death and regeneration redeemed. Beyond the 'partial vision' of time-bound consciousness there is a 'dying' that opens the door onto truth: for then perception brings to its aid a faculty of the Divine—as we see in 'The Betrothal':

> I must die first, to look into those eyes,
> And yet no lover ever found his bride
> But with that look. Brave children were denied
> Until I saw the grave where faith must rise
> Out of this dust.

Here, in the 'intervals of time' where, paradoxical to common sense, one sees with 'closed eyelids' and listens to 'tongues that are silent,' is the condition of man's ultimate freedom. Here to quote again from Coomaraswamy, 'It is not by the means of this All that he knows himself, but by this knowledge of himself that he becomes All.'

Clearly Watkins's life and work were that of a Christian. It is central to his vision that time, in its anthropomorphic significance, is envisaged in terms of the mercy of the Divine Love as the completion of knowledge and the redemption of man's natural estate. This theme, if not the explicit subject of any one poem, often forms the submerged point of imaginative coherence, at once the genesis and goal of a poem: for instance, of 'The Healing of the Leper', 'Touch With Your Fingers', 'Earth and Fire', 'The Instant' and 'Quem Quaeritis?' in which the 'narrow dwelling' of 'Him who has overcome the tomb'—the temporal death that embraces the infinite life—provides man with the 'greatest room'. Again, paradoxically, it becomes true that to the extent man is bound by the utmost commitment to perception of that 'stubborn and ornate' order of particular things by which he is surrounded and rejecting abstraction, the more he becomes free. For the poet the coterminous nature of humility and free-will are the precondition of the creative act itself:

Verse tests the very marrow in the bone,
Yet man, being once engaged by song, is freed:
The act itself is prayer, deliberate in its speed

He wrote that in 'The Interval', and he knew it from many years of meticulous and exacting craftsmanship.

In 'Unity of the Stream' the image of the poet's inspiration being 'like water from a fount' cannot fail to recall Plato's description that the inspired poet is 'like a fountain which gives free course to the rush of its waters' (*Laws* 719c). It ought to be a rehearsal of the obvious to point out that the bulk of Watkins's verse exemplifies the Platonic and traditional view that art is a mode of visionary perception in so far as contemplative experience provides the context of its inspiration—an intuitive power that is prior to any form of reflexive thought, as these lines from 'The Coin' affirm:

Vision, where the fountain fell,
Masters more than time can tell.

Not by reason or by sense
Alone, can words be made intense,

But by this, alive and dead,
Breaking from the fountain-head.

NOTES

1. This theme is explored in greater detail in the author's *Vernon Watkins: Inspiration as Poetry, Poetry as Inspiration* (Temenos Academy, London, 2002).
2. Plotinus, *The Enneads*, translated by Stephen Mackenna (London, 1962), pp. 58–9.

Epiphanies of Light

KATHLEEN RAINE'S POETIC VISION HAS TWO PREVAILING LEIT-motifs. By the inclination of the poet's temperament, it is a poetry of spiritual nostalgia (a quality it shares with the poetry of Edwin Muir) on the immemorial theme of the descent of the individual soul into the world of mundane generation. By instinct of vision it sees in the particularity of nature an image of the infinitude of the divine presence. The Judeo-Christian myth of the Fall, Plato's myth of the Cave, and the Neoplatonic myths of Demeter and Persephone especially, and of Cupid and Psyche might all be said to contribute to her imaginative themes each in its way casting a luminous shadow over the poet's vision. The subtle contours of at least one of these mythical structures is hardly ever wholly absent from any poem.

This is not 'nature poetry'—outward appearances seen with eyes of flesh. Potency of image and depth of theme in this poetry appeal to powers beyond nature. Here, the poet's eye leaves the least trace possible of the psychology of the observer on what is observed. For all their incarnational qualities these poems seldom reconstruct a physical context between the seeing 'I' and its relationship with some observed scene, with all the psychological and optical continuities that such a relationship suggests in common experience. More often than not, nature is here presented as a series of 'snap-shot' images: a tree, a bird, a stone, a shaft of light, with the immediate context or qualities described very often with the utmost brevity, as, in 'April's new apple buds', for instance:

April's new apple buds on an old lichened tree;
Slender shadows quiver, celandines burn in the orchard grass—
This moment's image.

or in '*That flash of joy*—'

> Like scent of budding leaves borne on the wind,
> Or pure note, clear,
> Heart trembles to, like water in a glass,
> Like a flame that bows and leaps
> As sound-waves pass.

Nature is perceived in the poet's eye as a series of individual points or nodes of cognition. Natural appearances do not stand as a reality outside and beyond the eye of the poet. Both nature and imagination are part of one and the same dynamic process. The perception of nature is not treated as a description of objects in physical space so much as a series of images invoking an inner, qualitative apprehension, each image gathering to itself something of the numinous presence of every image seen as a theophanic totality. For this poetry, such is the pattern whereby the divine principle is indwelling in each thing. The observer is thus the pre-fallen Adam or soul, the eternal moment of cognition at one with the essence of all named things. Each particle of nature's world, minute or vast, is itself the 'perfect signature' of what it is, while at the same time it is 'the everywhere and nowhere invisible door' opening onto the hidden presence beyond the threshold of being from whence we may discern and contemplate its sacred mystery. Thus the poet's eye does not look outwards into the distance of space in order to evoke or initiate the concatenation of semblances that nature 'seems' to be, but looks inwards with the eye of the heart to the qualitative space of imaginative perception, where nature's forms are the occasion for a recollection of their archetypes—their paradisal origin. Were it not for this transparency of phenomena the theophany that is the world would be a totally bewildering prison of unintelligible multiplicity.

It is also important that we grasp the many modalities of the 'I' in these poems, for their boundaries and identities are ever shifting from poem to poem—even, on occasion, from line to line. Except where

obviously autobiographical—the 'me', for instance, in 'Heirloom'—
the 'I' of the poems is rarely that all too readily assumed 'ego' for, by
the terms of the poet's imaginative vision the 'ego' is no more than
an inferred—'soul lonely comes and goes' ('Lachesis')—localisation of
outward behaviour:

> I, who have become
> What I am,
> Am what I have done,
> Free-will has come to this.

As ego the 'I' is unreal and unknowing as an individual identity. So the
question arises, what degree of reality can be ascribed to that 'I' who is
the poet? A question posed by this short poem:

> Do I imagine reality
> Or does the real imagine me?
> Unimaginable imaginer
> What part does the imagined play?

It is the omnipresent, omnimodal essence that is the theme, for
instance, of 'The Poet Answers the Accuser' and of 'Dissolving Identity':

> As if permeable—it seems
> Body no longer bounds my times and places,
> Past and future merging in the measureless
> Abundance, not much or little, but all—
> Mountains, waterfalls, leaves, seas,
> Clouds, birds, skies, whatever is,
> The marvels of the shabby commonplace
> Suffice for the *mysterium* to indwell.

The ultimate reflecting surface of conscious perception that knows
all that is known—'of these I am the I' ('*Blue butterflies' eyed wings*')—both

153

makes knowledge possible and in 'Named' is the indefinable person-hood of the soul:

> Yet by that unknown knower I am known
> And who I am . . .

and in 'To the Sun' is all that is known:

> Who am I who see your light but the light I see
> Held for a moment in the form I wear, your beams.

Finally, then, the soul's 'I am' is God's consciousness that looks out at the providential 'good' of the Creation, as in 'Seventh Day':

> Every natural form, living and moving
> Delights these eyes that are no longer mine
> That open upon earth and sky pure vision.
> Nature sees, sees itself, is both seer and seen.
>
> This is the divine repose, that watches
> The ever-changing light and shadow, rock and sky and ocean.

As the 'I' is specifically the organ of essential vision it is the soul's apprehension of the world of creaturehood, the mundane realm whose vesture it has here donned. But it is also akin to a divine presence whose descent into Soul is to open the eyes of cognition, so that when it is stirred by the diversity and riches of the outer world of appearances, the eyes of imagination perceive those outer appearances in the light of their original purity. For though the perceiver, like those souls enchained in Plato's Cave, is obliged to watch shadows only, those shadows are created by the light that gives them what substantial life they have—that one same light from which the soul itself descends and which is never entirely lost to its remembrance. The actions of the soul are by definition, and by the terms of the poet's imaginative vision, explicit qualities of cognition.

So, in the beginning, we open our eyes and are conscious of a 'reality' that invites us to know it. That is already the wonder of wonders, at once the profoundest mystery and the simplest action, as in the short poem:

> I've read all the books but one
> Only remains sacred: this
> Volume of wonders, open
> Always before my eyes.

This mystery, this act, addressed in part four of 'To the Sun', is already in some sense a state of illumination since it participates in the light of cognition that is not only the being of all we know but is also the light by which we know it:

> Not that light is holy, but that the holy is the light—
> Only by seeing, by being, we know,
> Rapt, breath stilled, bliss of the heart.

Only the opacity of our habitual, bodily state prevent us from seeing the constant myriad epiphanies that comprise the book of nature—the world before us.

We are, then, caught in the pattern of a cosmic dream that dreams the soul's descent into that least substantial thing, the world perceived by a reflective consciousness, a theme perfectly encapsulated in this short poem:

> World:
> Image on water, waves
> Break and it is gone, yet
> It was.

From the deep interiority of the cosmic dreamer dream itself emanates to become the preformal essence of things; the 'thought' of the dream becomes a hidden language at the root of every named thing, whose meaning we are and whose ultimate significance, enquired of in these lines from 'Dream-Flowers', is the inscrutable light of the Logos.

> There is a speech by none in this life spoken,
> Yet we the speakers, we the listeners seem;
> In that discourse, all signifies:
> But what mind means the meaning that then is known?

So it is, from the initial point of illumination there dawns a consciousness, an 'I' who knows, a creature of time, faced with the outward flow of nature's attractions themselves demanding to be re-cognised. In multiplicity the original One is compromised, is dismembered and scattered; essential unity is, in 'Natura Naturans', both veiled and revealed by the multiple and becomes movement:

> Veil upon veil
> Petal and shell and scale
> The dancer of the whirling dance lets fall.
> Visible veils the invisible
> Reveal, conceal
> In bodies that most resemble
> The fleeting mind of nature never still.

With the descent of the soul into the lower world there comes the burden of consciousness of self, the realisation that the world of multiple 'seeming' is but a shadowy replica of the paradisal world above, sullied by the presence of fallen man, as in the last section of 'Eileann Chanaidh':

> Because I see these mountains they are brought low,
> Because I drink these waters they are bitter,
> Because I tread these black rocks they are barren,
> Because I have found these islands they are lost;

Upon seal and seabird dreaming their innocent world
My shadow has fallen.

This is a poetry, then, not of what befalls the retina—a recording of
Nature 'natured', it is a vision of that abiding, invisible *Natura* con-
cealed in every appearance, that insubstantial source of the original
wonder. In 'The World' it is called 'nothing':

> It burns in the void
> Nothing upholds it.
> Still it travels.
>
> Travelling the void
> Upheld by burning
> Nothing is still.
>
> Burning it travels.
> The void upholds it
> Still it is nothing.
>
> Nothing it travels
> A burning void
> Upheld by stillness.

And yet, because it is no-'thing', this worldly habitation of the soul
must be accorded the status of illusion, as in '*Say all is illusion . . .*':

> Say all is illusion,
> Yet that nothing all
> This inexhaustible
> Treasury of seeming,
> The blackbird singing,
> The rain coming on,
> The leaves green,

> The rainbow appearing
> Reality or dream
> What difference? I have seen.

Only by way of this 'seeming' can we come to recognise the numinous presence that upholds what *is*! For what other reason should it *be* at all? We cannot come to know the Presence without first knowing the outward appearances of things, and we know it in such measure as we know ourselves, the agent of knowing itself—knower and known articulations of the same reality as in 'Self':

> Who am I, who
> Speaks from the dust,
> Who looks from the clay?
> . . .
> Who out of nothingness has gazed
> On the beloved face?

This is the dramatic leitmotif of the poet's vision, the soul's fall from the paradisal vision of childhood innocence—its native Edenic realm—and not its exile in the domain where things are born, suffer and decay, this prison of generated nature where all is circumscribed by death. As so often in the poems—in 'Eudaimon' for instance—it is a matter of communication between the poet, the will of the soul, and her Daimon the visionary inspiration of the soul's utterances.

> Bound and free,
> I to you, you to me,
> We parted at the gate
> Of childhood's house, I bound,
> You free to ebb and flow
> In that life-giving sea
> In whose dark womb
> I drowned.

> In a dark night
> In flight unbounded
> You bore me bound
> To my prison-house
> Whose window invisible bars
> From mine your world.

And so the soul comes to seem entirely claimed by the nature it has assumed in the existential flux, the 'natal waters' (in 'Message from Home') that all but submerge it. In rock, in flower, in wind, in the loved human face, enamoured of all these things in which it comes to recognise itself, it shares a common love that binds all things to one another—the theme of 'Message':

> Look, beloved child, into my eyes, see there
> Your self, mirrored in that living water
> From whose deep pools all images of earth are born.
> See, in the gaze that holds you dear
> All that you were, are, and shall be for ever.
> In recognition beyond time and seeming
> Love knows the face that each soul turns towards heaven.

The soul's love is not only a bond that unites all things. In each thing it sees itself as the underlying substance of that thing. It is a love that moves the soul to descend to the utmost particle of the mundane world, even to the point (in 'Exile'), where it all but seems that the gulf dividing its own nature from what is 'other' is conquered:

> Their being is lovely, is love;
> And if my love could cross the desert self
> That lies between all that I am and all that is,
> They would forgive and bless.

The soul undertakes this radical descent or participation, so that a witness to the love that joins all things becomes evident, as in 'Message From Home':

> Of all created things the source is one,
> Simple, single as love; remember
> The cell and seed of life.

Earlier in the poem it is spoken of as a knowledge of all things; the soul, being all that it knows, takes on the qualities of that which it knows:

> Do you remember, when you were first a child,
> Nothing in the world seemed strange to you?
> You perceived, for the first time, shapes already familiar,
> And seeing, you knew that you had always known
> The lichen on the rock, fern-leaves, the flowers of thyme,
> As if the elements newly met in your body,
> Caught up into the momentary vortex of your living
> Still kept the knowledge of a former state,
> In your retained recollection of cloud and ocean,
> The branching tree, the dancing flame.

So it is that the identity of the soul, within this alien abode, is never complete, never becomes total, (in 'The Invisible Kingdom') for it always retains some memory, some intimation of its origin beyond the play upon the senses that is the nature of sensory reality:

> We know more than we know
> Who see always the bewildering proliferating
> Multiplicity of the common show.

Yet it cannot escape the term of its exile among that which it also knows as an ensnaring illusion. For that reason it is subject to all the sufferings and perturbations of this labyrinth of darkness that is its

mortal state. What the soul has knowledge of in its generated embodiment is just such as prevents its returning (in 'Yes, *it is present all, always*')
to all that it originally is:

> ... these
> Blind, ignorant, sealed senses shut me
> From all I love, long for, know and am.

In the third of 'Three Poems of Incarnation', the soul's descent is
spoken of as a transgression, as if against a mother's counsel not to
trespass beyond the precincts of its true abode:

> Go back, my babe, to the vacant night
> For in this house dwell sin and hate
> On the verge of being.

But if soul does not descend how shall body be redeemed?

> I will not go back for hate or sin,
> I will not go back for sorrow or pain,
> For my true love mourns within
> On the threshold of night.

The poet's burden is to unfold the drama of the soul's trial of wandering within the kingdom of partial forgetfulness, of partial remembrance, of visionary occlusion, the accustomed sensory world that has
powers of imprisonment to immerse the soul in a world alien to its
original purity, an impediment that delays its return, as these lines
from 'Story's End' show:

> O, I would tell soul's story to the end,
> Psyche on bruised feet walking the hard ways,
> The knives, the mountain of ice,
> Seeking her beloved through all the world,

Remembering—until at last she knows
Only that long ago she set out to find—
But whom or in what place
No longer has a name.
So through life's long years she stumbles on
From habit enduring all.

Implicit in this same delay of entanglement is the knowledge that the soul's mortal journey becomes itself a strand, a skein from which the fabric of suffering and joy, dark and light, birth and death, is woven. That is to say, perception itself takes on something of the veil of nature's appearances, itself puts on the fabric of illusion, for like is only known by like. Such is the theme of 'Into what pattern . . .':

Into what pattern, into what music have the spheres whirled us,
Of travelling light upon spindles of the stars wound us,
The great winds upon the hills and in hollows swirled us,
Into what currents the hollow waves and crested waters,
Molten veins of ancestral rock wrought us
In the caves, in the graves entangled the deep roots of us,
Into what vesture of memories earth layer upon layer enswathed us
Of the ever-changing faces and phases
Of the moon to be born, reborn, upborne, of sun-spun days
Our arrivals assigned us, our times and our places,
Sanctuaries for all love's meetings and partings, departings
Healings and woundings and weepings and transfigurations?

No less part of the fabric are those other souls whom we have known and loved, partly known and partly caused to suffer in the blind search for identity, and who, in the knowing have become part of the one woven substance of all, as 'Threading my way . . .' tells:

Threading my way, devious in its weaving
Into the web of the world,

Time's warp running from far back, and on
Of lives, crossed life-lines, intercrossed, entangled,
Knotted, knitted together, ravelled, unravelled,
Hidden, re-emerging in new design,
Always growing, unseen or seen
Patterns we make with one another, distant
Or near, from immemorial past
Into unbounded future running unbroken,
Threads so fine and subtle of lives
We weave and interweave, slender as light,
Intangible substance of the age-old
Ever-extending all, makers and made
Who feel the pull of love, of grief, on every thread.

The passage of 'time's warp' delays the soul's tread from ascending the path of return to its native realm. For the soul, time is the 'measure of absence' from the now-ever of its timeless self that is in turn the measure of the perpetual flux, the ever-weaving vesture of begetting and dying that offers no abiding sanctuary, as in 'The Halt':

Travelling in trains of time, succession and causality
From sleep to sleep, from dream to dream we pass,
Desire from day to day drawing us on
But never bringing to our abiding-place,
For with our exiled selves we everywhere remain.

This 'absence' is not a measurable 'distance' that divides the soul from its native country. As spoken of in 'The Elementals', it is nothing other than 'a curtain, veil or door/A mist, a shadow, an image, or a world . . . through the thinnest surface', assuming 'guises and transformations', a procession of super-essential lights become corporeal, playing upon the surface of time.

The more we attempt to grasp this 'apparent' reality, the more paradoxical it becomes, for though it exists in time ever moving and changing, it never is any 'where' or 'when', so that the warp and woof of our perceptions in time, woven into the memories of what we recall, actually become the substance of that transient world—a world we make and remake in perception. Here is the theme in the third part of 'A Departure':

> It winds into the heart
> That unbroken thread
> From present to past,
> Without to within
> From seen to seer,
> Sky, garden, tree, bird
> Transmuted, transposed
> To memory, to pain
>
> . . .
>
> Become what I am
> Who am the sum
> Of all I have lost,
> Who am the maker,
>
> . . .
>
> I am my past
> And future approaching
> Days unknown.

But hidden in the very heart of each perception is that which is not subject to time's flow, is unmoving, is unconfined by time and place, indeed is that place (spoken of here in 'Monessie Gorge') where time is robed with living experience:

> 'I am the stream', I said:
> And yet not I the seer,
> The running water,
> The joy unbounded.

This, the still centre of our being, the Soul of the soul as it might be called, is the very condition of our witness of all manifestation and change: 'There is stone in me that knows stone' ('Rock'). It is the core of every perception that spans the measureless divide between future and past, that smallest aperture, the 'needle's eye' of the timeless that 'spans the heavens to find the punctum out' ('The Hollow Hill'). It is the axial root of being in 'The Elements':

> From height to depth, circumference to centre
> The primal ray, axis of world's darkness
> Through all the planes of being.

That same axial ray of light sends an arrow of illumination into the heart of darkest matter. The punctum is in particular the 'moment', the ever-now eye-view of many of the poems, in which all things as distinctly perceived become part of the soul's living garment of experience, as in 'The Moment':

> To write down all I contain at this moment
> I would pour the desert through an hour-glass,
> The sea through a water-clock,
> Grain by grain and drop by drop
> Let in the trackless, measureless, mutable seas and sands.

That implicit order, the soul's true being, is imprinted in the shapes, patterns and rhythms of nature. It can be conceived as a series of archetypal forms that move through time-bound things, as a dynamic rhythm of energy that passes through the sea to shape the waves. Themselves unmanifest, they configure the proportions and qualities of manifest forms as 'shaped on the day of creation' ('Shells'). Their labour is to be 'ever the weaver of roses' ('Rose'). The soul's return is also, then, a return to an identity with the archetypal order, a restoration of 'one who before my days was beautiful' ('High Summer'): the beauty of earthly things is finally traced back to Beauty itself.

If its radical innocence is 'joy unbounded' what then is grief, the soul asks, for surely it is real? And what could it be but the pain of severance. For having come to know earthly desire, it must now relinquish its grasp upon what it has come to hold dear. Such love (in 'A Departure') has no choice but to embrace what it desires; the more desirable for the knowledge that the object of its love must pass away:

> 'It is their transience makes dear
> Places and days that once were home,
> Sheltering refuges of earth
> Nearest at heart when they are gone,
> Faces we do not see again;
> Is it not death that seals our love?'

Thus the soul gathers up the fragments of its mortal life, its temporary attachments made here on alien earth, in preparation for an ascent to the intelligible realm where the meaning and worth of their transience ultimately resides. In this realm—the abode of Demeter awaiting her Persephone—all souls are returned to the ever-present eternity of their being—from 'Monessie Gorge' again:

> Live on in me, remembered ones,
> I am your future and your memory
> Who, within this ever-moving now
> At rest in change, wore, as I wear,
> The seamless dress of earth and sea and sky.
> One in the long unbroken flow
> We who have been are one another for ever
> Whose voices to the stars must cry and cry
> In sorrow and in ecstasy, 'I am'.

Persephone returns to Demeter, which is to say the soul, now beyond time's depredations, is at one with its higher faculties and is thus able to perceive those mutable semblances it has left behind as presences 'with power, beauty and awe'; that is, in their 'abiding essences' ('The Elementals'). In terms of the poet's vision of nature, the journey of earthly travail ends at the point where the threshold of the soul's native country begins, end and beginning indivisible as a single point of numinous vision, as in 'The Return':

> I have come back to ancient shores where it is always now.
> The beautiful troubled waters breaking over the skerry
> On the wind in sprindrift blown like lifting hair,
> Clouds gathering over the summits of Rhum in the clear blue
> Are as they were
> When long ago I went my way in sorrow.
> Time, measure of absence, is not here.

The return is the soul's remembering itself back into its own essential being so that it may be more fully and abundantly itself after its confinement and its dispersal among the 'teeming myriad' seeming of the natural world. In terms of the poet's imaginative vision, we have to transpose the journey as one into the very heart of physical reality, for it is this poet's rare gift to speak of the timeless essences while holding on to a vision of nature that neither makes of it a remote abstraction nor finds in it an occasion for sentimental reverie. This is at all times a poetry of incarnation in which it is crucially important to acknowledge that in the soul's return to the paradisal state from whence it has fallen—which is also to say in and through the spiritual cognition of nature—physical things of the sensory domain are not banished to some imagined limbo as if redundant and replaced by a new or alternative 'reality'. Here nature is redeemed *in its nature* by a fullness of vision that penetrates to the miraculous core of Being itself.

The thin veil of forms torn asunder, the bridge crossed from shadow to luminous source, the *re*-cognising of the mortal and natural as an epiphany of light—the simultaneity of all these is (in 'To the Sun'), finally, the art of self-identity:

Ancestral sun, do you remember us,
Children of light, who behold you with living eyes?
Are we as you, are you as we? It seems
As if you look down on us with living face:
Who am I who see your light but the light I see,
Held for a moment in the form I wear, your beams.

. . .

Presence, terrible theophany,
Am I in you, are you in me,
Infinite centre of your unbounded realm
Whose multitudes sing Holy, Holy, Holy?
Do you go into the dark, or I?

For the poet the question must remain. It was Yeats, as has been earlier remarked, who said that the saint goes to the centre but the poet stays at the circumference where all things come round again. Kathleen Raine's poetic vision embraces the sacred incarnation of nature as mirroring the holy epiphany of the soul's intuitions. In the consonance of seer and seen the poetic image here serves to express a vision that is at one and the same time universal and particular, descriptive and analogical, combining meticulous observation with precise invocation. The immemoriality of her vision of the soul's function articulates what the soul was created to know. Which is to say that the poet invokes the more-than-human from the threshold of the human, as in 'The Poet is of those':

The poet is of those
Who see but cannot be
In that holy place.

Vision of mirage trembles
In a dry wilderness
Of an elsewhere island.

Of garden and tree I have told,
Mountain and clear stream,
Remember, who may not enter
That ever-present kingdom
Where some I know and have known
Have been and are always.

Whose brightness from far away
Shines on my desert journey:
Yet I bear witness.

For what purpose the witness but to conjure a vision of the innate
perfection of the unknowable on which all things rest. These poems
celebrate the theophanic immediacy of truth and beauty present in the
instantaneity of pure perception. And the shadow also. For the absence
of that purity of vision is the incompleteness of all worldly knowledge,
the sorrow and distance of 'otherness' in human experience. When
the purity of the soul's vision is restored, the nature of reality and the
reality of our nature is nothing less than the face of the eternal spirit
that looks out at us as we look into the panoply of wonders before our
eyes—from 'The Invisible Kingdom':

Yet unceasing
The music of the spheres, the *magia* of light,
Spirit's self-knowledge in its flow

Imaging continually the all
Of which each moment is the presence
Telling itself to the listener, the seer in the heart
Contemplates in time's river
The ever-changing never-changing face.

In the final section of 'To the Sun' the poet describes the actual
experience of her visionary intuition, an initiation that has proved to

be the pre-formal mould into which by far the major part of her imaginative expression has been poured:

> not in the seen but in the seer
> Epiphany of the commonplace.
> A hyacinth in a glass it was, on my working-table,
> Before my eyes opened beyond beauty light's pure living flow.
> 'It is I,' I knew, 'I am that flower, that light is I,
> Both seer and sight.'
> Long ago, but for ever; for none can un-know
> Native Paradise in every blade of grass,
> Pebble, and particle of dust, immaculate.
> 'It has been so and will be always', I knew,
> No foulness, violence, ignorance of ours
> Can defile that sacred source:
> Why should I, one of light's innumerable multitude,
> Fear in my unbecoming to be what for ever is?

Eden's Native Ground

THE EBB AND FLOW OF THE ONE CURRENT OF LIFE, INFORM-
ing the pattern of births and deaths that is the interlinking of all generations, is the background against which Wendell Berry's poetry unfolds.
We notice the stubborn refusal to employ 'artifice' or 'fancy' (Coleridge),
in an almost meagre linguistic discipline that lends a note of tenacity
to the poet's diction. A hard-won integrity relates directly to the poet's
day-by-day life where the mental rigour of the writer is balanced by
the physical rigour demanded by the life of a working farmer. There
is hardly a poem by Berry that is not resonant with the consciousness
of a life lived according to this sense of weighing the active and the
contemplative in terms of one another. Here is the poetic record of a
daily life *made* deliberately so as to balance the consumption of physical resources with the creation of spiritual reserves. And conversely,
reserves of physical exertion are measured against the assimilation of
spiritual resources. Given this integrity of vision of the life of man's
work and prayer in intimate association with the land, with equal
necessity we note the poet's conception of the place of man in the greater
order of reality which reaches beyond man, that larger 'nature' in which
he is immersed and of which he is a part.

In his poems Berry explores life as it has been lived by all men, except
for those who, for whatever reason, have lived their life at some remove
from the physical and spiritual sources common to all men in all ages.
In other words his recurrent theme is man's primordial relationship
with the land—the perennial world of his natural habitat. The theme
is briefly and unambiguously stated in 'Rising':

> And that is our story,
> not of time, but the forever
> returning events of light,

> ancient knowledge seeking
> its new minds. The man at dawn
> in spring of the year
> going to the fields . . .

This is Adamic man, seen here in terms of those elementary values native to the American tradition of rural life and writing and which, notwithstanding their denial in the predominantly urban culture of contemporary America, remain an enduring part of the consciousness of the American people.

Berry's 'Adamic man' is continually in possession of a clear and direct experience of nature. His vision is uncluttered with the accretions of cultural history except insofar as nature itself is the living depository of man's interaction with the land. Berry goes to some lengths in his agrarian essays to show how human culture shapes and provides the 'instructions' by which man either cooperates with or challenges the land.

Of the land itself there are three sorts or conditions: between the extremes of that wildness which is untouched by any human intervention (and which was the sacred home of the North American Indian) and the land which man cultivates, there is that 'marginal' land that has suffered the deprivation, in whatever form, of a human culture out of touch with, if not deliberately opposed to, its ecological constitution. Man's cultivation of the land may bring to birth one sort of potentiality for spiritual renewal. Wildness brings another in which man has played no constructive part. But it is in man's irresponsible intervention that the co-ordination of human and natural rhythms falters and men learn the extent of their dependence upon the larger 'nature', as well as the consequences of their ability to create a heaven or a hell on earth. In the Sabbath of 1980 'The intellect so ravenous to know' we find:

> All orders made by mortal hand or love
> Or thought come to a margin of their kind,
> Are lost in order we are ignorant of,

Which stirs great fear and sorrow in the mind.
The field, if it will thrive, must do so by
Exactitude of thought, by skill of hand,

And by the clouded mercy of the sky;
It is a mortal clarity between
Two darks, of Heaven and of earth, The why

Of it is our measure.

For the 'Adamic spirit', so to say, nature is self-evidently the 'good' that God sees it to be at the Creation. But for the poet that good is qualified as often as not by the realisation of human guilt at the rejection of the wisdom of the fields that from the beginning of the 'new-found land' has been part of the American way of life. (Kathleen Raine, writing of Berry, has remarked that the colonisation of America was western man's 'second chance' with nature.) But in both cases the indigenous ecological wisdom of the native inhabitants was effaced. The 'Adamic spirit' and the turning away from the land (perhaps too vast and wild to comprehend) seem permanently to co-exist in the American mind. It is the recurrent theme of the loss of the Edenic vision that haunts all of Berry's poetry. It might even be said to be the ultimate occasion for all of his writings.

The world
is a holy vision, had we clarity
to see it—a clarity that men
depend on men to make.

This 'holy vision' in which man might come to discern the features of his responsibilities and place in the order of created things has its symbolic sanction in the biblical verse: 'The invisible things of him from the creation of the world are clearly seen, being understood by the things that are made'. The two primary motifs of the poetry in which this theophany is participated are the cycles of the seasons, with their parallel cycles of human generation reaching back into the past and anticipated for the future, and the revelation of light. One would expect a farmer to be aware of the changing qualities and gradations of light, both through the times of the day as well as the varying seasons. And so it is that for Berry the life of the seasons and the beings that inhabit them are so many modes and patterns of the intangible light of the spirit made incarnate. As all natural growth feeds on solar light (call it photosynthesis if you will), so men see by the light of intelligence: in the common substance of light in which all life is sustained, life is seen as life. Organic growth and spiritual growth, being now external, now internal, are modes of the one same interpenetrating light descending to be incarnate in the sap of plants no less than in the veins of men, returning in the subtle fire that is literally the 'light of life' that 'cometh down from the Father of lights'. These processions and transformations are for Berry 'works of light'. In one of the 1986 Sabbath poems, we find:

Slowly, slowly, they return
To the small woodland let alone:
Great trees, outspreading and upright,
Apostles of the living light.

Patient as stars, they build in air
Tier after tier a timbered choir,
Stout beams upholding weightless grace
Of song, a blessing on this place.

They stand in waiting all around,
Uprisings of their native ground,
Downcomings of the distant light;
They are the advent they await.

Receiving sun and giving shade,
Their life's a benefaction made,

And is a benediction said
Over the living and the dead.

In fall their brightened leaves, released,
Fly down the wind, and we are pleased
To walk on radiance, amazed.
O light come down to earth, be praised!

Whether stated or implied, the symbol of light has here to be understood in many subtle gradations of meaning as it is applied to the ever-changing nuances of mood and context in the poems. For instance, in 'Hail to the forest born again', another Sabbath poem, the image of light appears four times. But further resonances of the symbol are also present in such words and phrases as 'born again', 'Heaven-invading fire', 'its forms', 'clarity', 'fellow presences' and 'out of nothing':

Hail to the forest born again,
that by neglect, the American benevolence,
has returned to semi-virginity, graceful
in the putrid air, the corrosive rain,
the ash-fall of Heaven-invading fire—
our time's genius to mine the light
of the world's ancient buried days
to make it poisonous in the air.
Light and greed together make a smudge
that stifles and blinds. But here
the light of Heaven's sun descends,
stained and mingled with its forms,
heavy trunk and limb, light leaf and wing,
that we must pray for clarity to see,
not raw sources, symbols, worded powers,
but fellow presences, independent, called
out of nothing by no word of ours,
blessèd, here with us.

In these poems the theophany that is the Creation is the *face* of the Creator's love, making, as the poet has written in his essay 'The Gift of Good Land',

> the ultimate mysteriousness of Creation a test of intellectual propriety and humility . . ... The Creator's love for the Creation is mysterious precisely because it does not conform to human purposes. The wild ass and the wild lilies are loved by God for their own sake and yet they are part of a pattern that we must love because it includes us. This is a pattern that humans can understand well enough to respect and preserve, though they cannot 'control' it or hope to understand it completely. The mysterious and the practical, the Heavenly and the earthly, are thus joined.

It is the signature of all Berry's work to seek the impress of unchanging stability within the evolving patterns of mutability. The all-pervasive presence in the poems is the image of the light of eternity, in this instance broken, as it were, into the spectrum of recurring, seasonal generation. As with the image of light itself, the hidden ground of permanence and fixity is very often the 'hidden ground' of the poem itself, not present as a distinct image, but all the images of the poem being suspended in it. In the last section of 'Rising' it is so.

> Ended, a story is history:
> it is in time, with time
> lost. But if a man's life
> continue in another man,
> then the flesh will rhyme
> its part in immortal song.
> By absence, he comes again.
>
> There is a kinship of the fields
> that gives to the living the breath
> of the dead. The earth

opened in the spring, opens
in all springs. Nameless,
ancient, many-lived, we reach
through ages with the seed.

Again, as is so often the case with the image of light, the pivotal
image around which the procession of changes revolve, is all the more
powerfully at work in the poem by virtue of its being understated. The
poems of The Wheel perhaps most perfectly exemplify Berry's vision of
the ever-changing lights of the theophany as a circle, a wheel, or a
dance, even, as in the passage quoted above, as a song, choired by the
multiplicity of things. In 'Our Children, Coming of Age' the whole
substance of the poem is pulled together into a meaningful shape—
like iron-filings patterned within a magnetic field—by the unnamed
'hidden' punctum ('That ghost who stirs in seed and womb') that is the
eternal, creative source of life.

In the great circle, dancing in
and out of time, you move now
toward your partners, answering
the music suddenly audible to you
that only carried you before
and will carry you again.
When you meet the destined ones
now dancing towards you
we will be in line behind you,
out of your awareness for the time,
we whom you know, others we remember
whom you do not remember, others
forgotten by us all.
When you meet, and hold love
in your arms, regardless of all,
the unknown will dance away from you
toward the horizon of light.

Our names will flutter
on these hills like little fires.

Since the 'mysterious and the practical are joined', part of the cyclical theophany has to do with the minute interactions of people with their material place on earth. In the attachment of people to the primary sources of their well-being as spiritual and physical beings, is nourished the integrity of the body's transubstantiation of sunlight, soil and rain. In the sixth section of 'The Clearing', the poet speaks of this, the proper activity of work, where the physical, the aesthetic and the spiritual are conjoined, and where the daily death and rebirth of the flesh reveals the pattern of meaning:

> As the vision of labor grows
> grows the vision of rest.
> Weariness is work's shadow.
> Labor is no preparation
> but takes life as it goes
> and casts upon it
> death's shadow, which
> enough weariness may welcome.
> The body's death rises
> over its daily labor,
> a tree to rest beneath.
> But work clarifies
> the vision of rest. In rest
> the vision of rest is lost.

In that rest from which our bodily work arises and to which all our efforts return, the opposites cohere and inform one another with a vision of what is greater than any division can show. We recall that God rested on the Sabbath from the work of the Creation the better to see the good that was its glory. It is through this contemplative stillness they continually invoke that these poems are best approached. Indeed, this stillness, the true source of wonder, lost in work, found in rest, lost and found again, is the fruitful joining of the earthly body and the spirit of inspiration. When the vision of the conjoint reality, greater than either of its parts, is denied, the song that is the harmony of creation's every part goes unheard. It is required of man that he be attuned to the alternating rhythms of nature the better to resonate with the order that is the Creation as God's handiwork. Here is the theme concentrated in one of the poet's 1980 Sabbaths.

> Six days of work are spent
> To make a Sunday quiet
> That Sabbath may return.
> It comes in unconcern;
> We cannot earn or buy it.
> Suppose rest is not sent
> Or comes and goes unknown,
> The light, unseen, unshown.
> Suppose the day begins
> In wrath at circumstance,
> Or anger at one's friends
> In vain self-innocence
> False to the very light,
> Breaking the sun in half,
> Or anger at oneself
> Whose controverting will
> Would have the sun stand still.
> The world is lost in loss
> Of patience; the old curse
> Returns, and is made worse
> As newly justified.
> In hopeless fret and fuss,
> In rage at worldly plight
> Creation is defied,
> All order is unpropped,
> All light and singing stopped.

If, in his practical involvement with the earth, man is able to unite with nature to the degree he can come to know himself as having a common destiny with it, that is not because of the sentiment nature is capable of inspiring in him, but because the intelligence of man—the organ by which he knows beyond reason—and the order of nature share in the intelligence of the Creator.

> The wheel of eternity is turning
> in time, its rhythms, austere,
> at long intervals returning,
> sing in the mind, not in the ear.

This self-knowledge is a re-cognition of the primordial wholeness and unity. We may know it by the divisions and opposites of the created world; the world of particular and discrete entities, of contrasts that exclude one another, of unreconciled elements. These *are* the world. But in our love of the beauty of the order they *re-present* abides the original wholeness, the love of the Creator for his Creation. At the heart of our joy in the perception of each thing comprising the Creation we draw together the divisions without which there would be no perception of it, and thus no occasion for love. Often present, the theme is explored in these lines from the fifth section of the early poem 'The Design of a House':

> If reason was all, reason
> would not exist—the will
> to reason accounts for it;
> it's not reason that chooses
> to live; the seed doesn't swell
> in its husk by reason, but loves
> itself, obeys light which is
> its own thought and argues the leaf
> in secret; love articulates
> the choice of life in fact; life

chooses life because it is
alive; what lives didn't begin dead,
nor sun's fire commence in ember.

Love foresees a jointure
composing a house, a marriage
of contraries, compendium
of opposites in equilibrium.

The reasoning mind may experience things at some remove on the basis of probability, but our certainty of the grace and gift that is the continuity of the incarnating light is evident in our perception of the world of wonders before our eyes. 'For the Future' captures in a few deft strokes the essence of the matter.

Planting trees early in spring,
we make a place for birds to sing
in time to come. How do we know?
They are singing here now.
There is no other guarantee
that singing will ever be.

There is no room for romanticism in Berry's approach to nature. His vision of the commonality of the earth and the body precludes those emotional states that mere surface appearances can inspire in passive imagination. If, as he states in 'The Clear Day',

The ground's the body's bride,
Who will not be denied

then in a further sense the earth is also man's discipline, even though his 'marriage' to it is only consummated beyond the sphere of his direct involvement with it. The theme is all-pervasive throughout the work but especially so in the Sabbath poems. Let this one from 1979 illustrate:

Enclosing the field within bounds
sets it apart from the boundless
of which it was, and is, a part,
and places it within care.
The bounds of the field bind
the mind to it. A bride
adorned, the field now wears
the green veil of a season's
abounding. Open the gate!
Open it wide, that time
and hunger may come in.

Much of Berry's polemic in his prose essays is directed against the worst depredations of the agribusiness mentality in its approach to the land, where just such as this reciprocity between the body and the earth is destroyed. The direction of their polemical thrust is by no means absent from the poems, though they are far from being pro-grammatic of the argument. But a subtler range of possibilities is allowed for in the poems that have by turns now a benevolent, now an exultant, now a paradoxical voice, among others. For his paradoxical vein the poet has invented the persona of the Mad Farmer. He is a sort of Holy Fool who flourishes in the interstices of failed conformity and lifeless authority —dead officialdom in its many guises. His wisdom has been won by persisting in his folly. He is the Lord of misrule and insurrection in an age of conforming, blinkered complacency. His wis-dom is given its head in 'Manifesto: The Mad Farmer Liberation Front'. It is at its most trenchant in 'Prayers and Sayings of the Mad Farmer', and in 'Mad Farmer in the City' he identifies himself with Mother Earth, whose nascent music he discerns awakening under the cracked pavements and the thrusting angles of the cityscape. Anybody who has felt themselves besieged by the corporate or governmental mandarins of the status quo might take comfort from Berry's alter ego.

The Mad Farmer poems stand out in relief from the body of Berry's poetry in that they articulate an overtly humorous note seldom present elsewhere. Berry drops his guard of restraint reluctantly, favouring, in general, a stance of meditative seemliness, utilising his unremittingly plain diction. Commenting on this Michael Hamburger, in his introduction to *The Landscape of Harmony*, makes a pertinent observation: 'It is in his poetry, therefore, that he takes the greater risk—not that of being misunderstood, but that of being understood too well and too easily, thus of being rejected both for what he says and for disdaining the ambiguities that would make for a "suspension of disbelief" in those who do not accept what he is saying.'

The plainness of diction goes hand in hand with a noticeable propriety of style, both of which are accounted for in the poet's belief that the art and discipline of making poems 'informs us of our human nature' such that if the poet is to preserve the integrity of their source he is called upon to respond with an appropriate dedication and responsibility to the fact of his humanity. In this way poetry is lead out of the circle of the artificiality of its means to embrace the wider community of values so that it might once more attempt to 'tell the truth'. Berry's propriety, therefore, comes from a concern for what poetry is *for*—a proper sense of its occasion as a means of making the 'necessary connections' that subsist between truth, language, nature and the community of man. In the sobriety—at times even austerity—of his linguistic resources, therefore, Berry achieves the greater freedom that is the polar opposite of self-inflated subjectivity. In his 'Notes: Unspecialising Poetry', Berry has stated: 'When a poet takes himself as his subject, he leaves out propriety altogether. He does not know the difference between what is appropriate and what is interesting, or the difference between what interests him and what interests everybody . . .. By taking oneself too seriously one is prevented from being serious enough'. And in his major essay 'Poetry and Place' he also comments: 'To be trapped in one's own mind is insanity . . .. To be trapped in another person's mind . . . is imprisonment'.

It is of the nature of his seriousness that this poet should so seldom deploy the more obvious linguistic felicities of poetry-making in order to seduce the ear of the reader. In the seemliness of their tone we see, as it were, the reflection of the poet's attempt to be faithful and worthy, without destruction, diminishment or falsification to the order of values from which true poetry must be nourished if it is to have any life beyond the means of its making.

Berry's special mastery is that, by means of his preferred diction and chosen propriety of style, he is so often able to achieve a mood of rapt and purified observation that evokes the numinous essence of the visible, as these lines from 'Thrush song, stream song, holy love' from the Sabbaths of 1982 testify.

> Design
> Now falls from thought. I go amazed
> Into the maze of a design
> That mind can follow but not know,
> Apparent, plain, and yet unknown,
> The outline lost in earth and sky.
> What form wakens and rumples this?
> Be still. A man who seems to be
> A gardener rises out of the ground,
> Stands like a tree, shakes off the dark,
> The bluebells opening at his feet,
> The light a figured cloth of song.

Berry's range is narrow and deep. His poetry does not function on the level of descriptive nature poetry. And he is to be clearly differentiated from the ecologists for this reason. Man cannot appeal to his human superiority over the world of nature other than through a sanction for his 'humaneness' in what transcends him as a human being per se. This is equally true of that 'idolatry' of nature which is the weakest expression of romanticism, as it is of the pretence that an ecological appeal to the well-being of the biological sphere represents the attainment of transcendent values. It is not that these attributes are wrong, but that they are incomplete and therefore dangerous to the degree they might mask the fact that any recovery of the sacred quality of nature inextricably involves at the same time the spiritual destiny of man, 'created in the divine image'. The desacralisation of nature has been effected by human secular culture. Wendell Berry's poetic vision reminds us of this.

> When field and wood agree, they make a rhyme
> That stirs in distant memory the whole
> First Sabbath's song that no largess of time
> Or hope or sorrow wholly can recall.
>
> But harmony of earth is Heaven-made,
> Heaven-making, is promise and is prayer,
> A little song to keep us unafraid,
> An earthly music magnified in air.

He has preferred to base his imagination at the earthly end of the polarity of heaven and earth, avoiding disembodied spirituality on the one hand and the abstraction of intellectualism on the other. If his vision of the world of men and nature is true, it is so by virtue of its recognition of the ultimate metaphysical nature of both—its acceptance of the fact that all we know is surrounded by the mystery of the unknown.

> Best of any song
> is bird song
> in the quiet, but first
> you must have the quiet.

Index